WILLIAM P. LYONS MASTER'S ESSAY AWARD

The William P. Lyons Master's Essay Award was established

in 1960 by the Department of History

of Loyola University, Chicago,

and the Loyola University Press.

The Award is made annually

to encourage significant work at the Master's level

in history in American universities.

It recognizes scholarship

that is exemplary in style and method,

based solidly on original sources

and interpretatively significant in current research.

1961

Staughton Lynd
Anti-Federalism in Dutchess County,
New York

1962

Herbert Alan Johnson
The Law Merchant and Negotiable Instruments
in Colonial New York 1664 to 1730

Midwestern Books Competition 1963
American Institute of Graphic Arts Fifty Books of the Year 1964
Society of Typographic Arts 1964

1963

Charles H. Harris, III
The Sánchez Navarros: a Socio-economic
Study of a Coahuilan Latifundio 1846-1853

Midwestern Books Competition 1964

1964

No publishable manuscript submitted.

1965

David Paul Thelen
The Early Life of
Robert M. La Follette 1855-1884

1966

Jack D. Ellis
The French Socialists and
the Problem of the Peace 1904-1914

WILLIAM P. LYONS MASTER'S ESSAY AWARD 1967

DAVID W. SOUTHERN

The Malignant Heritage:
Yankee Progressives
and the
Negro Question
1901-1914

To end slavery was to commit the nation permanently to an ideal that might prove humanly unattainable. . . . Here was the showdown, not to be understood at once, not to be accepted for generations, but nevertheless, wholly inexorable.

Bruce Catton,
This Hallowed Ground

The problem of the twentieth century is the problem of the color-line.

W. E. B. DuBois,
The Souls of Black Folk (1903)

DAVID W. SOUTHERN

The Malignant Heritage:
Yankee Progressives
and the
Negro Question
1901-1914

LOYOLA UNIVERSITY PRESS

Chicago, Illinois

1968

About this book

The Malignant Heritage: Yankee Progressives and the Negro Question 1901-1914 was designed by William Nicoll of Edit, Inc. It was set in the composing room of Loyola University Press. The text is 12/14 Bodoni Book and the notes, 8/10. The display type is 12 Bodoni Book caps.

It was printed by Photopress, Inc., on Warren's 60-pound English Finish paper and bound by A. C. Engdahl and Company, Inc., in Bancroft cloth.

PREFACE

I wish to acknowledge my debt to Thomas F. Gossett whose book *Race: The History of an Idea in America* supplied me with ready and indispensable information. Also C. Vann Woodward's monograph *The Strange Career of Jim Crow* was extremely useful for writing the introductory chapter on the triumph of racism. In addition I wish to thank Professors David L. Smiley and Richard L. Zuber of Wake Forest College who have read the manuscript and have offered valuable suggestions for its improvement. And not the least of my gratitude goes to Dianne King and my wife Judith who together typed and proofread the manuscript. Of course, errors of fact or interpretation are strictly my creation.

DAVID W. SOUTHERN

Wake Forest College

vii

CONTENTS

ix

x

INTRODUCTION

In the 1960's liberals stand in the vanguard of the Negro civil-rights movement. But liberals of this century have not always been racially tolerant, much less inclined to embrace the cause of Negro rights. In fact, the progressive movement, the first great liberal movement of the twentieth century, was unmistakably caught up in a powerful tide of racism. Between 1890 and 1910 the South capitulated to the ranting and raving of white-supremacy demagogues. Southerners began disfranchising, segregating, and lynching Negroes with a vengeance. Coincident with the anti-Negro campaign in the South came a deluge of racial violence and the tragic phenomenon of American

1

twentieth-century democracy: the voteless, victimized, and thoroughly vanquished Jim Crow Negro.

Since the innovation of Jim Crowism and the rise of progressivism were contemporary events, one might conclude that the two were destined to clash in spirited combat. Negro leaders of the time so reasoned. Negro hopes quickened at the assumption of national leadership by Theodore Roosevelt, an accidental president who seemed possessed of a genuine concern for the much-maligned Negro. Moreover, progressivism, sweeping irresistibly over the political landscape from 1901 to 1914, once again raised the banners of humanitarianism. Energetic progressives spoke fluently the Jeffersonian idiom of egalitarianism, promising social justice for all men. In modern-sounding political jargon, they championed human rights over less worthy property rights. But, as the Negro soon discerned, such hopes and promises were no more than a will-o'-the-wisp when they met the color line—a line that had been drawn in every geographical section and in every facet of American life.

The many terrorized and disgruntled southern Negroes who sought refuge in northern cities during the Progressive era found no relief from violence and omnipresent discrimination. They also found that northern progressives offered no plan of social redemption for their oppressed numbers. An aspiring white middle class condemned the malefactors of great wealth, but they failed to condemn the great malefactors of race who sought eternal degradation of the Negro. The trenchant fact was that the overwhelming majority of northern progressives had acquired a racial philosophy akin to that of the Negro-baiting politicians of the South. The only difference was that the racism of the northern progressives was often more circumspect, more subtle. It was no subtlety, however, that the end of the Progressive era saw the Negro at the very nadir of his harried existence.

Looking back, it is tragically evident that the major blind spot of the progressives was the Negro problem. Furthermore,

2

historians of the Progressive era have failed to reveal adequately the seamy side of its racism and to evaluate the implications of its failure to respond to the acute grievances of the Negro.[1] Thus this study.

The urgent and increasingly explosive nature of the Negro civil-rights movement today is not so inscrutable in light of the shabby civic treatment afforded the black man by supposedly liberal statesmen of this century. Instead of searching for ways to bring the Negro into the full citizenship of American life and all of its promise, progressives only compounded what was to become one hundred years of post-Civil War neglect and miscalculation concerning the Negro. In the present times, political liberals and moderates have cooperated to pass significant civil-rights legislation; but considering our ominous racial heritage and the increasingly long and hot summers in our cities, one worries whether the attempts to placate the Negro have been too little, too late.

This study makes no pretense of completeness. For such a broad and variegated movement as the progressive movement, time and expense prohibited the examination of every potentially valuable source. What follows, then, I believe, is a representative view of progressive thinking about one of our most lasting and perplexing problems.

THE TRIUMPH OF RACISM

When in 1901 President Theodore Roosevelt entertained Booker T. Washington, the famous Negro leader and educator, as a dinner guest at the White House, incensed southerners unleashed a caustic rhetorical barrage. "Entertaining that nigger," raged South Carolina senator Ben Tillman, will ". . . necessitate our killing a thousand niggers in the South before they learn their place."[1] For two months, in varied and scathing language, the southern press vilified Roosevelt and Washington for their blasphemous breach of social conduct. In the next decade southern mobs more than half filled Tillman's demanding quota.

The orgy of alarm raised by the Roosevelt-Washington dinner was symptomatic of the rampant and increasing racism in the South at the dawn of the new century. The changing attitude of the South was attested by the fact that Grover Cleveland, a Democrat, had several times entertained Frederick Douglass, predecessor to Booker Washington as Negro spokesman, at the capital without raising a furor—and Douglass had a white wife.[2]

The intense hatred of southern whites for Negroes prevalent in the early twentieth century was not, as commonly supposed, a direct heritage of the Civil War. This belief is typical of the gross misinformation about the Negro after 1865, and seldom do history texts throw any light on the subject.[3] The fact was that southerners did not have a comprehensive plan in regard to the Negro when by the Compromise of 1877 federal troops withdrew from the South. The extreme discrimination and excessive brutality that was the lot of the Negro from 1890 until the 1930's was not the case during the first twenty-five years after America's great internecine war. For instance, the Negro was not disfranchised until the late 1890's and the first years of the twentieth century. As late as 1901 North Carolina had a colored representative in the national Congress. Nor did lynching become identified as a punishment strictly for Negroes until nearly 1900. Moreover, there were forces which tended to protect Negro rights long after northern bayonets disappeared from the South.

One force that served to humanize the treatment of the Negro was the leadership of the conservatives or Bourbons who engineered the overthrow of the carpetbag governments. L. Q. C. Lamar of Mississippi and Wade Hampton of South Carolina were two examples of leaders in the "redeemed" governments who sought justice for the Negro. Lamar gracefully went about his Senate duties in Washington, sharing Mississippi's representation in that august body with Blanche K. Bruce, a Negro. When Bruce's Senate term expired, a complimentary speech by

5

Lamar helped to confirm him as Register of the Treasury.[4] Hampton was elected governor of South Carolina in 1876, returning that state to "home rule" after nearly a decade of carpetbag government. Hampton ran on a platform promising to accept the Thirteenth, Fourteenth, and Fifteenth Amendments in good faith; to administer perfect equality before the law to both races; to provide education for both races; and to accept the help of all, regardless of race or party, in establishing good government. His slogan of "free men, free ballots, free schools" was reminiscent of the Republican campaign of 1856.[5]

After winning the governorship, Hampton sincerely tried to carry out his campaign promises. In his first year of office he appointed over sixty Negroes to state offices. In general, he conducted race relations with wise consideration, enough so to be called a true statesman.[6]

To be sure, Hampton and his kind were the targets of radical Negrophobes; but for a time moderate men like Hampton largely controlled the destiny of the southern Negro. In early 1877 Hampton wrote President Rutherford B. Hayes: ". . . if Federal Troops are withdrawn from the State House, there shall be on my part, or that of my friends no resort to violence. . . ." Hampton then reiterated his campaign pledges of 1876 to reassure Hayes of his sincerity.[7] No doubt, Hayes honestly thought that justice for the Negro "could be got best and most surely by trusting the honorable and influential southern whites."[8]

More skeptical northerners, of course, did not trust the word of southerners to protect the freedman. In 1878 Thomas Wentworth Higginson, a suspicious northern abolitionist, toured the South to see whether southerners had some covert plan to reenslave the Negro. Higginson's patron saints were John Brown and General Ben Butler, the "Beast." As a soldier in 1861, Higginson wrote that the defeat at Bull Run was not at all discouraging because it pointed up the need of the government to make the war one of emancipation.[9] In 1878 Higginson found the acceptance and treatment of the Negro better in the South than in the North. Negroes were not segregated on trains or in other public conveyances. "How can we ask more of the States formerly in rebellion," he concluded, "than that they should be abreast of New England in granting rights and privileges to the colored race?"[10] When Higginson returned to the South in 1884, he found no reason to change his thinking.

In most cases, the conservative Democrats were little afraid of Negro domination. In addition, much of the old paternalism of master to slave remained in the new setting of the races. As to suffrage, Alexander H. Stephens, ex-Whig and ex-vice-president of the Confederacy, believed that it was impossible to disfranchise the freedmen, and that even if it were possible, it was not desirable.[11] In 1886 the Richmond *Dispatch* boldly asserted: "We repeat that nobody here objects to sitting in political conventions with negroes. Nobody objects to serving on juries with negroes."[12] Although federal troops left South Carolina to home rule in 1877 and the Supreme Court invalidated the Civil Rights Act in 1883, a state civil-rights law remained in South Carolina statutes until 1889 when it was repealed, not without a great deal of opposition.[13]

In the late 1880's and early 1890's there was a political resurgence of the Negro in many southern states. The agrarian discontent which culminated in the populist movement led to a bitter political fight between the Bourbons and the Populists. With the political division of the whites, the Negro held the deciding balance in the political tug-of-war. Therefore, whites of all political hues began to court the Negro voter. Tom Watson of Georgia, the best known of the southern Populists, campaigned for governor in 1892, denouncing lynching, Ku Klux Klanism, and injustices to Negroes. Watson needed the Negro vote to unseat the vested interest of Bourbon democracy.[14] However, the Bourbons were better manipulators of the Negro than were the agrarians. Bourbon planters and millowners marched their employees to the polls and voted them in gangs. Barbecue, beer, and whiskey were at the disposal of Negro voters. The total vote in Augusta was double the number of legally registered voters.[15] Not surprisingly, the outcome of the election was the defeat of Tom Watson.

Watson's failure to unseat the Bourbons was duplicated in many other southern states. The defeat of the agrarians on the national scene in 1896 was a decisive blow to populism. Not gaining their objectives, the Populists turned bitterly on the Negro, with whom they had always been hesitant bedfellows. The Bourbons, tired of buying Negro votes and stuffing ballot boxes, made an agreement with the Populists to eliminate the Negro from politics and let the white men fight their battles among themselves. With this tacit agreement of political rivals, "political niggerism" had run its course in the South.[16]

Mississippi led the disfranchisement movement by amending its constitution in 1890 to proscribe the Negro vote.[17] The "Second Mississippi Plan" made use of the poll tax, property qualification, literacy test, and understanding test. All of these tests white registrars could administer to the Negro voter with utmost discrimination. Between 1895 and 1910 seven other states followed the lead of Mississippi and amended their constitutions.[18] New devices appeared to circumvent the Fifteenth Amendment and to eliminate Negro voters without the disfranchising of more than a nominal number of whites. Most famous of these devices was the "grandfather clause" originated in Louisiana by which permanent registration was accorded those who had voted prior to 1867, together with their descendants.[19]

Southerners practiced no discrimination between literate and illiterate Negro voters. James Vardaman, senator from Mississippi, generously offered his view: "I am just as much opposed to Booker Washington as a voter, with all his Anglo-Saxon reinforcements, as I am to the cocoanut-headed, chocolate-colored, typical little coon, Andy Dotson, who blacks my shoes

8

every morning."[20] By 1901 when Virginia concocted a literacy test, white politicians found that Negro literacy was a distinct threat to their plans. One Virginian complained that half of the colored electorate could read and write.[21] When a reporter asked delegate Carter Glass, later a renowned senator, whether disfranchisement of the Negro was accompanied by the practice of fraud or discrimination, he replied: "By fraud, no; but discrimination, yes. . . . Why that is precisely what we propose; that, exactly, is what the convention was elected for—to discriminate to the very extremity of permissible action under the limitations of the Federal Constitution, with a view to the elimination of every Negro voter. . . ."[22]

The effectiveness of Negro disfranchisement was shown by the fact that in 1896, 130,344 Negro voters were registered in Louisiana. In 1900 there were 5,320 registered; in 1904 there were only slightly over 1,000 eligible colored voters.[23]

Had disfranchisement meant only the loss of Negro voting rights accompanied by betterment of race relations, perhaps it would not have become such a sad legacy. But the very nature of the most rabid disfranchisers and the methods they used caused an unprecedented deterioration of race relations. Along with Negro disfranchisement came the rise of the southern white-supremacy demagogues. These Negro-baiting orators were usually nonaristocrats of little education who capitalized on the Negrophobia of the lower-class whites to gain political office. "Pitchfork" Ben Tillman of South Carolina was a case in point. A journalist described Tillman as "a sallow-faced, shaggy-haired man with one gleaming, restless, angry eye."[24] A man of crude habits and defamatory speech, Tillman geared his campaign for the governorship in 1890 to the "plain people" of South Carolina. To the Charlestonian elite he sneered: "Men of Charleston, I have always heard that you were the most self-idolatrous people that ever lived; but I want to say to you that the sun does not rise in the Cooper and set in the Ashley. It

9

shines all over the state."[25] But castigating aristocrats was only half of his specialty; the other half was inciting the hatred of whites for blacks. In 1892, secure in the governor's chair, Tillman condoned mob violence: "Governor, as I am, I'd lead a mob to lynch a man who ravished a white woman. . . . I justify lynching for rape [of white women] and, before Almighty God, I'm not ashamed of it."[26] Tillman had his counterparts in Jeff Davis of Arkansas, James Vardaman of Mississippi, Hoke Smith of Georgia, and Charles B. Aycock of North Carolina— all impeccable proponents of white supremacy and of the Negro's degradation.

Along with the omnipresent shibboleths of Negro disfranchisement and white-supremacy crusades came promiscuous violence. There was perilous confrontation of the races in all facets of life. In 1898 in Lake City, South Carolina, Frazier B. Baker, a Negro, became postmaster. A few years earlier Wade Hampton had appointed scores of Negroes to office, but the appointment of Baker induced three thousand whites to send a petition to the postmaster general demanding his removal. When no action was taken, a mob gathered outside Baker's home and set it on fire. As Baker's wife and four small children fled from the flaming house, they were shot down. Baker was shot and left to burn inside the house.[27]

In the same year there were race riots in Greenwood County, South Carolina, and Wilmington, North Carolina, in connection with elections. In Greenwood County the rioting became so bloody that Senator Tillman (former governor) intervened and advised the whites to cease indiscriminate killing and to concentrate on the one family of Negroes that was guilty— that is, the family that had tried to enter politics.[28]

In the 1898 election at Wilmington, Aycock's campaign directors staged "White-Supremacy Jubilees" in which hundreds of armed men paraded the streets. "Pitchfork" Ben Tillman came up from South Carolina to lend a hand. White sympathiz-

10

ers from Richmond, Virginia, shipped carloads of guns and ammunition to Wilmington before the election. After the white-supremacy advocates had won the election over a highly frightened Negro electorate, a mob invaded the Negro district, killing twenty or thirty Negroes and wounding a large number. A Negro refugee insisted that hundreds of Negro bodies were dumped into the Cape Fear River. The leader of the mob received as compensation for the well-directed assault the mayoralty of the city.[29]

In Atlanta, Georgia, the election of 1906 brought on a massacre. In that year Hoke Smith, a conservative turned progressive, was running for governor on a platform to put the Negro out of politics. Tom Watson, once considered the savior of the Negro in Georgia, now supported the white-supremacy campaign as Smith's right-hand man. The Atlanta press in support of Smith played up lurid tales of Negro atrocities. The constant bombardment of infectious propaganda and election liquor plunged Atlanta into a sanguinary riot that lasted for three days. Following the common pattern, Negroes suffered many casualties and wanton destruction of property.[30]

The torrid pace of lynching from 1890-1910 told an ominous tale in itself. Surprisingly enough, between 1882 and 1888, 595 whites were lynched while only 440 Negroes experienced the same fate. However, by the last decade of the nineteenth century the emphasis of lynching had changed; lynching had become almost wholly a white sport and a Negro death warrant. In 1892, the apogee of lynching, 169 Negroes and 69 whites were lynched. From 1906 to 1915 ten times as many Negroes (620) were lynched as whites (61). Many of the Negro lynchings were characterized by crass brutality and fiendish torture. In 1893 in Paris, Texas, a Negro had his eyes gouged out with a hot poker before being slowly roasted to death.[31] Between 1891 and 1904, 25 persons were burned at the stake; all but two were Negroes (one a woman), the two exceptions being

Indians.[32] After lynchings, white youths in the crowds nimbly scrambled to get bones of mutilated Negroes to hail as proud souvenirs.

To southern racists the final ingredient in the ultimate solution of the Negro problem was a rigid system of segregation. The only law of the Jim Crow type in existence before 1900 was the segregation of railroad cars. South Carolina did not adopt such a law until 1898, again demonstrating the recent origin of Jim Crow legislation. Even then, the Charleston *News and Courier* was dubious about the law: "As we have got on fairly well for a third of a century . . . we can probably get on as well hereafter without it. . . ."[33]

After 1900, hospitals, restaurants, theaters, buses, elevators, insane asylums, prisons, rest rooms, and so on *ad infinitum*, were scrupulously segregated. Oklahoma ordered racially separate telephone booths. New Orleans separated black and white prostitutes. Atlanta perhaps won the separation-by-pigmentation game when it provided a "Jim Crow Bible" expressly for the colored witnesses swearing an oath in court.[34] Clarence Poe, editor of the *Progressive Farmer* (North Carolina), with the consent of the convention of the Farmer's Union, called for a law which would prohibit Negroes from buying land. Poe's panacea was to settle all the Negroes in two or three states of the deep South and move the whites out.[35]

Despite lip service given to "separate but equal" facilities, increased racism meant that facilities and opportunity for the Negro were becoming anything but equal. The expenditures for schools showed an increasing discrimination in education. During the years 1879-1880 under the leadership of Wade Hampton, expenditures for white and colored students were nearly equal—$2.75 for white and $2.51 for colored. In 1895, the year of disfranchisement, South Carolina spent only $1.05 on each Negro student and $3.11 on each white.[36] By 1911 expenditures were incredibly out of proportion, for in that year

$13.02 was spent on each white pupil and $1.71 on each Negro.[37] In a word, the state was spending 80 cents less on each Negro student in 1911 than in 1879, and spending $10.27 more on each white student. Such were the equalities of the "separate but equal" doctrine.

Southern white forces were not alone responsible for the triumph of racism in the South. The advent of a new Negro leader also facilitated the ease of the capitulation. Until his death in 1895, Frederick Douglass had served as spokesman for the Negro. Douglass was an exslave who had escaped before the Civil War and had become important in the antislavery movement in the North. He was an eloquent and tireless advocate of first-class citizenship for the Negro. However, with the death of Douglass there was a change in Negro leadership and, as a corollary, a pronounced change in Negro philosophy.

In 1895, Booker T. Washington became undisputed leader of the Negro by virtue of a carefully planned speech delivered at the Atlanta Cotton Exposition. Washington's intent was to appease the North, South, and the Negro—a highly improbable task in which he gloriously succeeded.[38] In his historic address at Atlanta, Washington told the racially mixed audience that the wisest people of his race knew that it was the "extremest folly" to agitate for social and political equality. Raising his hand aloft, Washington demonstrated the doctrine of segregation as he understood it: "In all things purely social we can be as separate as the fingers, yet one as the hand in all things essential to mutual progress."[39] In Washington's mind the only way for the Negro to win the respect of the white man was to forget his dreams of the ballot and social equality and pull himself up by his economic bootstraps. This economic formula meant simply doing the most common labor uncommonly well.[40]

Response to Washington's address was overwhelming. Startled southern leaders embraced Washington's philosophy of accommodation with unrestrained glee. Northern politicians, at

13

times still paying homage to Negro rights, grabbed the chance to dump the whole race problem into Washington's lap. The cordial respect accorded Washington by whites made him irresistible to the frustrated and confused Negro. Undeniably, Washington had the interests of his race at heart; but unwittingly he had played into the hands of the oncoming crop of racists just appearing on the southern political horizon. Economic equality, the one thing that Washington demanded, was denied the Negro. As it turned out, the harder the Negro worked, the more educated and efficient he became, the more he was discriminated against as being "uppity."

It was during the dark decades of Negro existence that Washington advised that the Negro work, learn, and win the respect of the white man. When Prince Kropotkin, a Russian revolutionist, heard that the Negroes had a conservative leader, he chortled, "What on earth do they have to conserve?"[41]

The final factor in the triumph of racism in the South was lack of opposition in the North.[42] Racism, an alleged disease of the South alone, was reaching epidemic proportions above the Potomac. In 1877 the formerly abolitionist New York *Tribune* reported that Negroes had proved that "as a race they are idle, ignorant, and vicious."[43] As some historians have pointed out, the Civil War took on a new dimension of tragedy when records revealed that often the abolitionists who passionately hated slavery and slave owners also hated Negroes.[44] The proposed Force Bill of 1890 was the last effort of the federal government to police racial affairs in the nineteenth-century South. This bill, which would have provided federal officers to supervise elections in the South, passed the House but failed in the Senate. In all probability the Force Bill was strictly a measure which the Republicans used to badger the Democrats into supporting a higher tariff bill, then pending in the Senate. Henry Cabot Lodge, sponsor of the bill, admitted that the House bill was "sold & sold for dishonest money," and that it was "a bare & miserable business." The Baltimore *Sun* saw the relationship of the tariff issue and the Force Bill as an evil bit of horse trading. Senator George F. Hoar of Massachusetts, who felt that the Republican party had to maintain its historic roots as the custodian of Negro rights, made an eloquent plea for the Force Bill in the Senate. The bill, nevertheless, failed in the Senate, becoming a major step in the national acceptance of Negro subjugation.[45] By skillful alchemy the Republicans had changed the reform Republicanism of Lincoln and Sumner to the more materialistic concepts of Marcus A. Hanna and Nelson W. Aldrich.

The few studies of the Negro in the North during the first decade of the twentieth century revealed that Negro life there was largely parallel to that of the Negro in the South. Inhabitants of Ohio expressed the opinion that the Negro was shiftless, unreliable, dishonest, and filthy. No Negro was allowed to reside or even stay overnight in Syracuse, Ohio.[46] Negroes were segregated in almost every facet of life, as in the South, save at the ballot box. The dominant complaint of the Negro in the North was that he did not get fair employment opportunities. The Negro had little success in joining labor unions. As Kelly Miller, an eminent Negro educator, phrased it, "The Negro is compelled to loiter around the edges of industry."[47]

Still the relatively more dangerous situation in the South caused many bitter Negroes to "vote with their feet." By 1910 there were 440,534 southern-born Negroes in the North.[48] The influx of Negroes increased racial tension in the northern cities. The result of emigrating Negroes in Springfield, Ohio, was a race riot, equal in blood and fury to the Atlanta massacre. Many Springfield Negroes, having fled from the South, refused to be passive any longer and began to arm themselves to fight.[49]

In addition to race riots, the popular literature was indicative of the new wave of racism. In 1901 a Bible publishing house in St. Louis released a book entitled *Is the Negro a Beast?* The book argued that the Negro was subhuman and possessed no soul. Therefore, it was of small consequence to kill him.[50] Thomas Dixon's trilogy of Reconstruction: *The Leopard's Spots: A Romance of the White Man's Burden 1865-1900* (1902); *The Clansman: An Historical Romance of the Ku Klux Klan* (1905); and *The Traitor: A Story of the Fall of the Invisible Empire* (1907) gained a wide audience. These books by a former Baptist preacher were the epitome of white-supremacy propaganda and the "black peril" school. In 1915 *The Clansman* was made into a popular film, *The Birth of a Nation*, which further stirred racial tension.[51]

With northern opposition silent or nonexistent and the Negro docile, radical southerners became openly defiant. Senator Tillman, to the dismay and embarrassment of his northern colleagues, boasted on the Senate floor: "We took the Government away. We stuffed ballot boxes. We shot them. We are not ashamed of it. . . . We called a Constitutional Convention, and we eliminated . . . all of the colored people. . . ." Tillman then shouted his conclusion: "The brotherhood of man exists no longer, because you shoot Negroes in Illinois . . . and we shoot them in South Carolina. You do not love them any better than we do."[52] A southern educator facetiously asked the question: "Does not the South perceive that all of the fire has gone out of the Northern philanthropic fight for the rights of man?"[53]

Certainly the transition from slavery to the caste system in the South had resulted in a grave deterioration of race relations. Furthermore, the North was quickly adopting the racial attitudes of the South. After studying race relations in America in 1906, William F. Bailey, Land Commissioner of Ireland, stated that he feared that there might be a gigantic race war if the Negro could find an adequate leader.[54] The race situation was perilous indeed.

In short, by 1900 racism had become an ominous wave of the future. Yet the first fourteen years of the twentieth century have not been remembered for their pervasive and militant rac-

16

ism or the abject disillusionment of nine million American Negroes. Rather, historians have filed these fourteen years under the more savory title of the "Progressive era," a period known for its enlightenment, optimism, and reforming zeal. Since progressivism and racism rode in on the same horse, one may well wonder how the two riders were related. Racists demanded the proscription of all inferior breeds of men; while despite Tillman's accusations, progressives demanded justice for all men. Whether this justice alluded to by the progressives extended beyond the color line was another matter.

THE PROMISE OF PROGRESSIVISM

Although faced with the onslaught of a rampaging racism as the twentieth century began, a number of Negro leaders looked to the new century with renewed hope. The main reason for that hope was Theodore Roosevelt and the spirit of progressivism that he seemed to transmit. Bishop W. Derrick, a Negro leader and clergyman, declared that Roosevelt had opened the "door of hope" to the Negro.[1] The event of the Roosevelt-Washington dinner in 1901 certainly seemed prophetic of better times for the Negro. Coincident with Roosevelt's rise to the presidency came the progressive promises of liberty and social justice which conjured up visions of Lincolnian grandeur to victimized Negroes.[2] Even W. E. B. DuBois, a severely skeptical Negro leader, acknowledged that there was a "renaissance of civic virtue" throughout the land; and he hoped that it might extend to the colored race.[3]

From 1901 until the culmination of the progressive crusade, there was a profound emphasis on human rights. Altruistic "isms" enjoyed the greatest popularity since before the Civil War. In 1912, expressing the spirit of the era, Woodrow Wilson presented to the public the sterling objectives of the New Freedom: "We have got to cheer and inspirit our people with sure prospects of social justice and due reward, with visions of the open gates of opportunity for all."[4]

The broad wave of reforming zeal that swept over the nation during the first two decades of the twentieth century was the commanding phenomenon of the time. Reformers attacked the parasitic corporation, corrupt politics, and the sullen discontent of millions of average Americans. The cup of civic virtue seemed to run over. With great abandon, progressivism mapped out an harmonious future that apparently applied to the bulk of Americans—even Negroes. Yet the simultaneous waves of progressivism and racism seemed not to jostle each other, but to ride in the same direction. Only a close scrutiny of the many-sided progressive movement could disclose whether it might serve as custodian for Negro rights. In a sense, both the race problem and progressivism were rooted in the Civil War.

Just as the Civil War willed America a perplexing race problem that emerged full-blown with the twentieth century, the economic seeds of the war grew into a great industrial complex that by 1900 threatened the tender roots of democracy. The Morrill Tariff, the National Banking Act, the Immigration Act, and the Homestead Act—all passed before Lee's surrender at Appomattox—had provided the tools of industrialism. Aided by a remarkably friendly Supreme Court, the Morgans, Rockefellers, and Carnegies had become the national directing forces.

19

From Ulysses S. Grant's administration to 1900, the rule had been big business and small politics, shrewd magnates and unessential politicians. The rich were stupendously so, and wealth found its way into the hands of a diminishing few. Economic liberty played havoc with human justice. In summing up the problem of industrialism, Walter Rauschenbusch wrote: "We have allowed private persons to put their thumb where they can constrict the life blood of the nation."[5] Corruption ran from the bottom of the political structure to the very top. In the Senate, the most powerful political body of the land, men were identified with the vested interests they served almost as surely as with the state they represented.[6] Urbanization had produced squalid slums, crime, and political bossism. This America was Theodore Roosevelt's inheritance when in 1901 by quirk of an assassin's bullet the young, energetic cowboy was kicked upstairs—to the presidency.

Had Roosevelt kept his pledge "to continue absolutely unbroken" the policies of his ill-fated, lackluster predecessor, the next four years would have been politically sedate.[7] However, Roosevelt was a keen opportunist, seemingly equipped with an infallible political barometer. He sensed the virile wind of social reaction sweeping over the nation, and he swayed gracefully with it.

The Progressive era, starting near the turn of the century and lasting until World War I, was characterized by a nebulous but potent impulse toward criticism and change of American life. William Allen White, an astute editor who felt the full vigor of the progressive force, perceived that after the Spanish-American War there was a great moral awakening in America. This arousing from iniquitous slumber revealed that America had moral qualms about its past greed and dishonesty.[8]

Whatever the origin of the progressive movement, it was not a philosophy easily expressed in wholly neat and logical maxims. Progressivism was an illusive, pragmatic affair mo-

20

tivated by sundry forces, a thousand small, obscure battlefields with fighting going on continually. So widespread and infinitely volatile were its movements that the whole creature was difficult to see. One historian who was seeking the essence of progressivism justifiably complained: "Never in the American past had so much been demanded in the name of so many whom so few could locate."[9]

Indeed, there are those who doubt that there was a Progressive era.[10] Roosevelt was a reluctant progressive whose attitude, at first, was "pragmatic and contemptuous" in response to reformism;[11] but being the politician that he was, he measurably changed his views by 1910. Woodrow Wilson, who was a Bryanphobe and wholly conservative before 1910, presented an equally enigmatic picture. An example of his high-sounding double talk was his statement in the *New Freedom* on corporate industry: "I am for big business, and I am against the trust."[12]

Unquestionably, big business was the midwife of much progressive legislation. Since businessmen were filling the party purses, they could dictate in many cases the boundaries of reform.[13] Amos Pinchot, biographer of the Progressive party (1912-1916), related that Frank Munsey and George Perkins, both irrevocably tied to the Morgan interests and the steel and Harvester trusts, were the *dramatis personae* in its formation. When Taft won the Republican nomination in 1912, Munsey and Perkins, after rapid-fire negotiations with each other, walked over to the dispossessed Roosevelt, and each laying a hand on his shoulder, said: "Colonel, we will see you through."[14] Perhaps big business manipulated progressivism more than progressivism manipulated big business.

Nevertheless, a majority of articulate thinkers from 1901 to 1914 advocated genuinely progressive measures; and many of the measures were passed, if in slightly modified form. Probably William Allen White summed up political progress in this period accurately by saying: "Capital is not eliminated from politics but it is hampered and circumscribed, and is not the dominant force it was ten years ago."[15]

Although the diversity of the progressive movement was enormous, generally it was concerned with three objectives: to regulate business and harness its power with a view to distributing wealth more evenly; to end corruption in government and make it more directly responsible to the people; to ensure social justice to the helpless and oppressed.[16] The method of obtaining these objectives was legislation. "He is really a Progressive," wrote Walter Owen, "who first discovers any wrongs and suggests the appropriate governmental action to prevent further abuse."[17]

No group more effectively pointed out the abuses in American life than the "muckrakers," as Theodore Roosevelt derisively dubbed them. Their reports always bordering on the sensational, the muckrakers found nothing too sacred for their prying eyes. They exposed the ills of American economic, political, and social institutions with biting pens. Back in the 1880's, writers such as Henry George and Henry D. Lloyd had warned of the dangers of corporate wealth; but they reached a limited audience. It was the ten-cent magazine, which appeared around 1900 and quadrupled the magazine-reading public, that afforded the muckrakers a proper vehicle for extensive advertisement of their wares.[18] The new magazines like *McClure's*, *Everybody's*, *Colliers*, and the *American Magazine*; and the older, more radical ones like the *Arena, Independent*, and the *Outlook* shocked the country with their sensational reporting.

Lincoln Steffens exposed the "shame of the cities"; Ida M. Tarbell pursued the Standard Oil Company; Ray Stannard Baker concentrated on the railroads. Jane Addams and Jacob Riis wrote plaintively of the slums and social vice. Upton Sinclair viciously attacked the meat-packing industry. Others turned to the problems of prostitution, the need for prison reform, literary immorality, and the like.

22

Political progressivism began its snaillike movements at
the local level and crept up to the national scene. Tom Johnson,
mayor of Cleveland during 1901-1907, was one of the best examples of a reformer at the local level. He cleaned out the
Hanna machine and fought for municipal ownership of utilities
and transportation, equalization of taxes, and efficient government. He recruited a competent staff of college-trained techni-
cians and intellectuals to help run the city. Johnson summoned
Frederic C. Howe, a recognized expert on city government and
a former student of Woodrow Wilson, to join the city council.[19]

Progressives were also making marked advances on the
state level. Robert M. La Follette, elected governor of Wisconsin
in 1900, set the pace of progressivism in the Midwest. For the
next decade or so Wisconsin was the proving ground for many
progressive experiments in government. La Follette's pet project
was the direct primary, which he felt would clean up political
bossism.[20] La Follette succeeded in curbing the power of the
railroads through taxation and rate fixing. He improved the state
civil service and initiated conservation of natural resources.
La Follette found his "brain trust" at Wisconsin University, his
alma mater. He often consulted eminent scholars such as Richard T. Ely, Edward A. Ross, and John R. Commons on matters
of government policy.[21] In 1906 "Fighting Bob," as La Follette
was called, went to the Senate where he became the leader of a
group of insurgent Republicans who castigated the old guard
and harassed Roosevelt for his inclination to compromise progressive measures.

Considering the fact that La Follette seldom compromised
on issues, he was an idealist. However, a more apt description
for him would be a "tough-minded progressive." La Follette
took staunch stands on separate issues, but he never gave a picture of what was the ideal society.[22] His watchwords were scientific research, efficiency, and pragmatism. He picked out one or
two issues at a time and fought diligently for them. He was no

great humanitarian affecting to have the blueprints of a perfect society. Frederic Howe, a contemporary reformer, confided that La Follette never made a statement concerning an issue unless it was grounded in meticulous research. His speeches were loaded with weighty statistics which added a hearty stamp of authority.[23]

La Follette's *raison d'etre* seemed to be to argue those particular problems which plagued the Midwest; of a larger view he was hardly capable. No doubt that was why he seemed so impertinent at times on issues of foreign policy. In domestic politics he wanted the end of monopoly and the renewal of competition, but he did not recognize an increasing part of society that could not compete. The direct primary was his solution to the problem of bossism, but he did not see any relation between destroying bossism and destroying slums. As to disfranchisement of millions of voters and abuse of Negroes, immigrants, and Indians, he was conveniently reticent.[24]

On the national scene, the year 1902 marked the initiation of progressivism.[25] In that year, President Roosevelt ordered the dissolution of the Northern Securities Company to begin. Also in 1902 the anthracite coal miners of Pennsylvania went on strike for a living wage. For the first time in American history the government recognized that there might be some justice on the side of labor. Roosevelt threatened the recalcitrant coal operators—who claimed that God was on their side—with sending in the Army to operate the mines. The threat worked.

During the coal strike, Henry Cabot Lodge wrote to Roosevelt and asked him: "Is there anything we can *appear* [italics mine] to do?"[26] To be sure, Roosevelt appeared to do more than he did. Domestically speaking, he spoke loudly and carried a small stick. But in the public's mind, Roosevelt had proved himself the opponent of the evil plutocrat. Trust-busting became linked with his name, and the progressives went to work with renewed confidence.

Until 1909 and the publication of Herbert Croly's *The Promise of American Life*, there was no comprehensive political theory of the ends and means of progressivism. Croly, an austerely intellectual, pathologically shy man, of small stature and pale complexion, supplied progressive theory in abundance. Attending Harvard intermittently for eleven years (without obtaining a degree), Croly had been imbued with the pragmatic philosophy of George Santayana and the reform-mindedness of Josiah Royce.[27] Croly's *Promise* placed him as one of the leading political philosophers of the twentieth century.

In a laboriously long book written in a style that at times lapsed into "rambling abstractness," Croly pleaded that the national body needed medical attention and a long-time supervision by "sanitary specialists." He suggested a positive type of government with a definite national purpose. In short, he wanted a Hamiltonian government pursuing Jeffersonian ends of egalitarianism. He warned that reformers must abandon the traditional "patriotic fatalism." "The national Promise," he said, "has been transformed into a closer equivalent of a national purpose, the fulfilment of which is a matter of conscious work."[28] Croly grasped for an element that would bring America a new kind of national cohesion.

More specifically, Croly did not demand an end to big business, but he demanded equally big government to cope with it. Like a majority of the progressives, he was suspicious of labor unionists. However, he did see the necessity of labor unions which would be regulated by the government (a kind of "Taft-Hartley philosophy"). Although Croly's national purpose included a mild sort of imperialism to spread democratic principles, he did not base his arguments on racist doctrines as did many other nationalists.[29]

The progressivism of Croly was dominantly a middle-class philosophy. It was the middle-class town and city consumer, a victim of rising prices and frozen wages, for whom Croly spoke.

He was not concerned with the plight of the impoverished, the much-abused labor leader, or struggling and oppressed minorities.[30] Croly addressed his message to over fifty million white, Anglo-Saxon Protestants who simply wanted a larger slice of the economic pie. Solid pragmatic philosophy showed that appealing to a small minority of the dispossessed would curb the overall effectiveness of the reform movement.[31]

Typical of the middle-class philosophy of the progressives was their attitude toward immigrants. By 1910 there were 13,345,000 foreign-born inhabitants in the United States.[32] A large percentage of these immigrants settled in the major cities, where political bosses thrived on their purchasable votes. The Anglo-Saxon bourgeoisie in the cities found themselves politically controlled by alien forces; therefore, one of the goals of the middle-class urbanite was to clean up political bossism. The northern city reformer constantly assailed the immigrant and blamed him for all political corruption, just as the southern reformer maligned the Negro and held him responsible for all political malfeasance. The former was called a progressive, the latter a demagogue.

In addition to the tough-minded view toward immigrants, a seamier side of progressivism was its infatuation with imperialism. America's rise to power stirred the hearts of many progressives, and with little philosophizing they added the doctrine of the "big stick" to their repertory of ideas.[33] Reasoning that our "little brown brothers" in the Philippines were unfit for self-government and other constitutional guarantees, it followed that our dark-skinned brothers at home should be kept servile.[34] The defense of imperialism often led progressives down philosophical paths forthrightly nonegalitarian.

By the time Herbert Croly had written his philosophy of progressivism, Theodore Roosevelt had retired from the presidency. As mentioned earlier, Roosevelt was a cautious progressive from 1901-1909, if one at all. After his maiden bluster in

1902, Roosevelt had become quite reluctant to stir up the political coals over further domestic reform. The Elkins Act and the Hepburn Act passed under Roosevelt were oft-divided loaves, as La Follette so loudly declared. Not without cause, progressives impugned Roosevelt's motives; but it is unlikely that progressive legislation could have passed with the old guard still entrenched in the Congress. Not until 1910 were some of the more intrepid conservatives removed from the legislature. In 1910 the insurgents finally succeeded in stripping the autocratic Speaker of the House, Joseph Cannon, of many of the powers which he had so masterfully used to stifle progressive legislation.[35] But possibly the most important occurrence of Taft's administration was that Roosevelt, off on a trip to Africa and Europe, packed a copy of *The Promise of American Life* in his bags.

In Croly's political treatise Roosevelt found the philosophy of government for which he had been groping during his political meanderings. No other book except Alfred T. Mahan's volume on the importance of sea power influenced Roosevelt's thinking so deeply. Returning from abroad in 1910, Roosevelt made a rousing speech in September at Osawatomie, Kansas, that was a prelude to the great progressive crusade of 1912. On the site where John Brown had written abolition in blood, Roosevelt announced that the government must enter positively into the cause of human justice. He stated that the "judiciary must be interested primarily in human welfare rather than in property." Unhesitatingly, Roosevelt also endorsed the graduated income tax, revision of the tariff, workmen's compensation, regulation of child and female labor, and stricter supervision of interstate commerce.[36] The garb of New Nationalism on the heretofore reform-shy Roosevelt appeared dangerously close to outright radical indecency.

As the election of 1912 drew near, there was a great drama of anticipation. Having forsaken Taft—or vice versa—the Republican progressives supported Roosevelt or La Follette, only to fail before a well-oiled Taft machine. At that point, Roosevelt, feeling "like a bull moose," leaped the political fence to what he thought were greener pastures and sired the Progressive party. The Democrats nominated a Johnny-come-lately progressive named Woodrow Wilson. The Socialist party nominated their perennial standard-bearer, Eugene V. Debs. With these candidates in the race, the year 1912 marked the flood tide of progressivism. All four party platforms were progressive; and three of four candidates were progressives—even crusaders.[37]

The campaign of 1912 came replete with an outpouring of progressive literature. Editors, intellectuals, and ministers availed themselves of the opportunity to interpret and direct the new political restlessness. Walter Weyl's *The New Democracy*, William Allen White's *The Old Order Changeth*, and Walter Rauschenbusch's *Christianizing the Social Order* were widely circulated. Although the emphasis of the progressive writing was on the trust problem, there was an added accent on social justice and human rights. Reminiscent of eighteenth-century liberalism, there was an increased optimism in the abilities of the common man to govern himself.

Pragmatism was still the watchword of progressivism, but there was an increased tincture of moral absolutism. Even the cold, calculating Croly observed that "little by little . . . the human race began to accumulate a fund of social virtue. . . ."[38] Walter Weyl, a distinguished progressive economist who later joined Croly and Walter Lippmann to publish the *New Republic*, asserted that the final objective of democracy was a social goal. "The basis of democratic striving . . .," he wrote, "is an ethical belief in the sanctity of human life, and the desire for an equality in this universal possession." Weyl insisted that democracy must be "open at the bottom," and must "cure" the slum or be destroyed by it; for depressed environments produced "social wrecks" that blighted the promise of America.[39] Weyl's progressivism was certainly of a warmer, deeper type than Croly's.

28

In 1912 religion entered politics more completely than at any other time since before the Civil War. Social gospelism, the religious phase of progressivism, preached that the proper sphere of religion was on *terra firma*.[40] Walter Rauschenbusch, a chief spokesman of the social gospelers, argued that the old religion lacked a "dogma of social redemption." The social gospel philosophy, as many interpreted it, was not far removed from socialism. Yet it advocated not the overthrow of capitalism, but the Christianizing of it.[41] In general, social gospelers concluded that there was a widespread shame and anger over oppression and "a new faith in human brotherhood."[42]

The Progressive party convention of 1912 was symbolic of the religious and humanitarian aura that surrounded parts of the progressive movement. The command was "Onward Christian Soldiers," for "we stand at Armageddon and battle for the Lord." William Allen White described the leader of the Progressive party as "a force for righteousness . . . because he had righteous people behind him."[43] The "Call" of the party read by the secretary of the convention summoned all persons "who believe in the right and capacity of the people to rule themselves, and . . . who hold that only through social justice and industrial justice . . . can honest property find permanent protection."[44] The opening speech given by Senator Albert J. Beveridge of Indiana brought pandemonium in the convention. Ever an eloquent orator, Beveridge declared: "We stand for a nobler America. We stand for a broader liberty, a fuller justice. We stand for social brotherhood against savage industrialism."[45]

The diversity of the participants whooping it up at the convention was immense. There were college professors, students, insurgent politicians, radical thinkers, disgruntled socialists, liberal clergymen, and "sharp-faced Southern politicians looking for a turn of the wheel that would let them fill their bellies long starved of patronage."[46] Everyone who had a cherished "ism" rushed to the "Bull Moose" party.

One unique group at the Progressive convention was composed of the social workers. Many of these young earnest altruists had abandoned the Republican party as a useless vehicle for attacking social problems of the age. Jane Addams, the most renowned of the group, gave a seconding speech for the nomination of Roosevelt. Judge Benjamin B. Lindsey of Denver, a trailblazer in the development of juvenile courts, also seconded Roosevelt's nomination. Though some social workers conspicuously distrusted Roosevelt, they stood pat on the Progressive platform. The platform—child welfare; the eight-hour day, six-day work week; the regulation of child and female labor; and a system of accident, old-age, and unemployment insurance—seemed to them the culmination of twenty years of struggle for social justice.[47]

To the voters of 1912, the choice between Roosevelt's New Nationalism and Wilson's New Freedom seemed very real. Presumably, Roosevelt stood for Hamiltonian government, Wilson for Jeffersonian. Some thought Roosevelt promised only to regulate the trusts, while Wilson—taking Louis Brandeis's advice that bigness was bad—proposed to destroy them.

In fact, the utterances of both Roosevelt and Wilson presented an extremely fuzzy picture of just where they stood. Already noted was Wilson's dubious stand on the trust question. Although the Democratic platform gave vent to its idea of strong states' rights, Wilson's New Freedom did not seem far removed from the New Nationalism concerning the role of the national government. Wilson said that "the law has to step in and create new conditions under which we may live. . . ." or, "whenever bodies of men employ bodies of men it ceases to be a private relationship." If Wilson masqueraded as a Jeffersonian, he spoke not of the "least government" but of "resolute government."[48] After Wilson had won the election in 1912, many Roosevelt worshipers admitted that the choice between Roosevelt and Wilson had been a matter of tweedledum and tweedledee.

30

On the subject of human rights, Wilson was without match for high-sounding humanitarian rhetoric. It is the duty of law, he said, "to see that every man has a fair chance to live and to serve himself, to see that justice and wrong are not wrought upon any." To the subject of the balance between property rights and human rights he addressed this sentence: "What I am interested in is having the government of the United States more concerned about human rights than about property rights." Wilson, too, showed his optimism in the abilities of the common man. "I believe, as I believe in nothing else," he beamed, "in the average intelligence of American people."[49]

Discounting business magnates and antediluvian conservatives, progressivism seemed to promise all things to all men (and women). Yet, the progressives were suspiciously equivocal or evasive on many twentieth-century problems facing them. One of these problems was the place of nine million Negroes subjected to a threatening wave of racism. Although many progressives wanted the extension of suffrage to women, they said little about the diminished suffrage of thousands of Negroes. Although they proposed to wrest the destinies of the many from the hands of the trusts, they said little about the fact that the South —and an increasing part of the whole nation—was a huge trust which denied the Negro his full rights as a citizen.

The problems of the twentieth century were new enough that progressive responses to them were singularly diverse and uninhibited. Thus the Progressive era, perhaps more than any other period, defied reduction into a neat bundle. Facing the problems of its time, progressivism—that uneasy mixture of materialistic pragmatism and humanitarianism—often appeared erratic. On the Negro problem, it was exceedingly so.

TOUGH-MINDED

PROGRESSIVE THOUGHT AND

THE NEGRO

Progressivism lacked clarity and consistency on many issues, and on the Negro question it lacked insight and integrity
as well. The congenital optimism that progressives had for the
common man did not extend to the Negro. The belief that all
men were capable of more participation in politics and worthy
of a fuller share of American opulence excluded nearly ten million persons of African descent. A movement striving for purifi-
cation of the ballot and a renaissance of civic virtue heartily
condoned the elimination of the colored man from politics.
While progressives promised to sign "a contract with the people," their definition of "the people" did not cross the color line.

32

At the flood tide of progressivism, northern liberals had come to view the Negro as "a permanent clot in the social bloodstream" of America.[1] Raised in the disillusionment of Reconstruction and confronted with race psychology and Malthusian economics, progressives, with few exceptions,[2] joined the swelling chorus of racism.

The progressives hastened to explain the Negro's low economic and educational status and high crime rate in terms of racial inferiority. They found it more expedient to heap abuse on the downtrodden colored man than to attempt to elevate him. Even though the Negro was but one generation removed from the influence of slavery and trapped in a revolving door of discrimination and oppression, the progressives claimed he had been given his chance and he had failed. The black man must now be left to the devices of the "best whites" of the South—those enlightened democrats schooled immaculately in divine-race theory. The fact was fairly obvious, however, that the "best whites" of the South seldom ruled on questions of race relations. Rather the Negro was subject to the debauchment of the "worst whites" —even in the North.

In short, a majority of progressives possessed a callous and inhumanitarian attitude toward the Negro and immigrant groups which they considered innately inferior. Much of the motivating force behind progressivism was in fact a "pride of blood," a feeling of Anglo-Saxon manifest destiny. As far as their attitude toward race was concerned—the Negro race in particular—progressives deserved the more precise label, "tough-minded progressives." They were tough-minded in that they were unfeeling and uncompromising in the face of obvious abuse of nearly ten million black Americans.

Perhaps the racial views of no other progressives were more significant than those of former abolitionists who were so vociferously instrumental in the freeing of the Negro. The career of these fitful humanitarians spanned three of American history's most traumatic eras—the Civil War, Reconstruction, and the Progressive era. The most notable features of these old Garrisonians were their rapid loss of ardor for Negro rights and the termination of their roseate dreams for Negro first-class citizenship.

Typical of this group was Lyman Abbott, a clergyman only twenty-six years old when the Civil War began. Two weeks before Lincoln issued his preliminary Emancipation Proclamation on September 22, 1862, Abbott demanded that Lincoln free the slaves. After waiting out the long war, Abbott ventured south to become executive secretary of the American Freedmen's Union Commission, a church organization for assisting the exslaves. As secretary of that organization from 1865 to 1869, Abbott saw in the Negro the latent ability to become a useful member of society. He marveled at the desire of the colored man to get an education.[3]

In 1867, after two years of service among the freedmen, Abbott prepared a report of his southern experiences entitled *Results of Emancipation in the United States* which was read at the international antislavery convention in Paris that year. He maintained that the "rapid and marked progress" of the Negro refuted "slavery's accusation of idleness and incapacity." Once, when a North Carolinian complained about racial integration in the schools, Abbott's office replied that discrimination because of color was "inherently wrong." In an article entitled "Equal Rights," he proclaimed that any pretense to white superiority rested on shadowy grounds. Above all, Abbott pleaded that the Negro must be given a chance to prove himself.[4]

After Abbott resigned from his position with the Freedmen's Union, he returned to his original vocation as a Congregationalist minister. In 1887 he became pastor of the great Plymouth Congregational Church in Brooklyn, Henry Ward Beecher's old pulpit, a position he held until 1899. Born with a political bent and reforming zeal, he became a leading exponent

34

of the social gospel movement in the last quarter of the nineteenth century. A prominent historian of the church wrote that "no leader in modern times has exercised a more abiding influence than Lyman Abbott."[5]

Giving in to his political and journalistic interests, Abbott had become editor of the *Outlook* in 1893 and had turned it into a powerful organ for progressive reform. In 1912 the *Outlook*, under his tutelage, became a mouthpiece for Theodore Roosevelt and the Progressive party. Politically, Abbott described himself as ". . . neither with the radicals nor with the reactionaries, but with the progressives in every reform."[6] Now with a flowing beard whitening with age, he had a patriarchal appearance; but despite his years, he was thoroughly abreast of twentieth-century life and its pressing problems. He believed that the people should rule themselves and that they would learn more quickly by their blunders than from the wisdom of an aristocracy. Abbott called for civil-service reforms, taxes to distribute the wealth, tariff reforms, and strict control of railroad corporations. He disclosed that it was "humanitarian indignation" that caused America to go to war with Spain in 1898. From his pulpit in Plymouth Church, reminiscent of "Beecher's Bibles" in Kansas, he preached: "I believe the proudest chapter in our history is that written by the statesmanship of McKinley, the guns of Dewey, and the administration of Taft." To Lyman Abbott the forcing of democracy upon the Filipinos was a divine mission; for "barbarism has no rights," he reasoned, echoing the language of Taney's Dred Scott decision, "which civilization is bound to respect."[7]

Now a jingoist democrat, Abbott had changed remarkably his attitude toward the Negro. Looking back on Reconstruction from the perspective of forty years, he reminisced: "It is easy . . . to see that men of that generation blundered egregiously, and brought upon the country, especially the South, and most of all upon the negro race, tragic disaster of their blundering."[8]

Nor did Abbott feel any longer that white superiority rested on shadowy grounds. Gone was his idea that the Negro would some day hold his own in society. The Negroes, he concluded, would continue to be an inferior and dependent people. In former times, Abbott wrote, there were three methods of dealing with inferior people: extermination, enslavement, or intermarriage. He realized that public sentiment disallowed the first two choices; and the third, he thought, was abhorrent. "For my part," he announced, "I thoroughly and heartily sympathize with the passionate resolve of the Southern people that this intermarriage shall not go on in their borders. . . ." He declared that the sentiment of "the highest and best men, the noblest and purest women" forbade it.[9]

Whereas Abbott had once been *persona non grata* in the South, he was now a popular lecturer there. "The Southerner," he explained, "understands the Negro better than the Northerner does and he likes him better."[10] Abbott reiterated Booker Washington's philosophy that the Negroes must be a people apart and must win the respect of the white man by bettering themselves educationally and economically. The rising economic status of the Negro would do more for him than all the "Northern interviews and Northern editorials on the rights of the Afro-American that have been spoken or written since the Proclamation of Emancipation."[11]

In 1903, before a joint meeting of the Orthodox and Unitarian Clubs in Boston, Abbott highly commended the six states that had added disfranchisement clauses to their constitutions. He scoffed at the argument that the amendments were meant to disfranchise the Negro. "Any man can vote, black or white, if he can read the English language, owns three hundred dollars' worth of property, and pays his poll tax," he contended. In order to vote, the Negro needed only these qualifications: "intelligence, thrift, loyalty."[12] To be sure, Abbott felt that the Negro had none of these enfranchising virtues.

Lyman Abbott was not alone in his racist conversion. Carl
Schurz was another former abolitionist whose later opinions on
the race problem were strongly at variance with his earlier
views. Schurz was one of the founders of the Republican party,
and he received a general's commission in the Civil War. During
the war, he was one of the few military men who enjoyed the
good graces of both Lincoln and the radicals. On November 14,
1861, he wrote to the "enlightened doctrinaire," Charles Sumner: "We must make up our minds to conquer the South as we
would conquer a foreign country."[13] Schurz believed that since
the South was fighting a defensive war, the North would become
demoralized *"unless* we avail ourselves of the only thing which
is sure to settle the business quickly and definitely. We *must*
proclaim the emancipation of the slaves."[14] Although he revered
Abraham Lincoln, Schurz admitted that in his political views he
was much closer to the radical Sumner than to Lincoln.[15]

In the summer of 1865, Schurz went on a mission for President Andrew Johnson to report the postwar situation in the
South. His findings were an acute damnation of Johnson's reconstruction. Schurz reported that the Negro was being held in virtual slavery in some parts of the South. He contended that the
life of the Negro, no longer worth a thousand dollars, was not
deemed "worth a wisp of straw." He added that all southerners
were against Negro rights and education; and should federal
troops vacate the South, it would swim in blood.[16] Schurz advised Negro suffrage as the only safeguard against white tyr-
anny. Any plan of educating the Negro before giving him the
ballot, he proclaimed, was nonsense; for the Negro would need
the ballot to secure an education.[17]

Schurz's report was undoubtedly colored by political motives, but it would be an injustice to charge him with indifference toward the Negro. In fact, he lauded the Negroes as the
only bright spots in the war-torn South. He was moved by their
lack of vindictiveness toward their former masters. To the

charge of Negro indolence, he replied that if anyone was lazy in the South it was the slavery-warped whites.[18]

But as it had affected the abolitionist Abbott, old age mellowed the attitude of Schurz toward the southern white and hardened it toward the Negro. In failing health, he visited Atlanta regularly where he made many white friends.[19] In 1903 he admonished President Roosevelt that southerners alone must carry on the battle against racism in order to disarm charges of "foreign interference."[20] Never again should Yankees make it their business to try to change the peculiar habits of the South. In 1904, two years before his death, he wrote in *McClure's* that the race problem defied solution. Race relations must be left to the southern "enlightened" whites.[21] Quite clearly, since his day as an abolitionist, Schurz had had second thoughts about the Negro.

Charles Francis Adams, Jr., was yet another abolitionist whose outlook on the Negro significantly changed during his long lifetime. As a young zealot from one of America's first families and as a Union officer, Adams viewed the Civil War as a divinely humanitarian crusade that banished the concept of "property in man" from the civilized world. Therefore, the war was well worth its exorbitant cost.[22] After the war, Adams wandered aimlessly in the profession of law and business, at one time serving as president of the Union Pacific Railroad. Being connected to the house of money changers bothered Adams's puritanical conscience. He found the business crowd "coarse, realistic, and bargaining."[23] In 1890 Adams escaped to his hometown in Massachusetts to write his father's biography and engage in reform politics.

In 1906, Adams's opinion on the Negro, absent in his *Autobiography* and papers, found lucid expression in an article printed in *The Century Magazine*. His attitude on race had crystallized as a result of a trip he had made to Africa. A view of the native land of the Negro brought about a candid reflection by Adams on the race problem. As he put it, at the sight of Africa, "the scales fell from my eyes." Gazing on the ancient city of Omdurman, he compared it most unfavorably with the cities of London and Paris: "As Omdurman is to London, so is the African to the Anglo-Saxon. Distinctly, the difference is too great to admit of measurement."[24]

African decadence brought Adams to ponder the "awful corollary" of what to do with nine million black Americans who could neither be expelled nor assimilated. It also brought about a condemnation of those reconstructionists who did their work "in utter ignorance of ethnological law." The race problem could only be solved when Americans approached it in less of "a theocratic and humanitarian, and more of a scientific spirit." Adams claimed that a political system could only work when applied to "homogeneous equals." The ignorant colored man only stalled the machinery of progress. Adams even doubted that the Negro deserved equality before the law, a position closely akin to that of the Vardamans and Tillmans. Like Abbott, he set aside as humanitarian rubbish the notion that the Negro was simply a man who had never been given a chance.[25]

In 1915, a year before his death, Adams wearied of working on history of the Civil War era. Perhaps prematurely, he judged that it was a period which had lost its impact on world history.[26] Such was the feeling of the erstwhile Garrisonians who now faced the new century. Abbott, Schurz, and Adams, all once in the vanguard of the struggle for Negro rights, had turned the Negro out just as surely as had the powers of the South.

One of the most conspicuous roles in the progressive drama was played by the muckrakers. This group flamboyantly and copiously attacked every conceivable malignancy of American life, whether it was moral, social, economic, or political; yet they were not visibly eager to investigate the Negro problem. Around the year 1905, however, Ray Stannard Baker, a well-known muckraker who had written prolifically on labor and the railroads, chose to examine the position of the Negro in American society. Baker traveled widely in the North and South, ferreting out facts and opinions concerning the status of the Negro. Most of these findings were printed serially in the muckraking magazines, primarily the *American Magazine*. In 1908 these articles were compiled into a book entitled *Following the Color Line*.

For a muckraker, Baker was surprisingly restrained in his evaluation of the race problem. His study was a thorough one and, as such, a devastating and frightful exposé of the naïve prejudice, absurd discrimination, and extreme racial tension that existed throughout the nation. But as far as progressivism itself was concerned, more revealing than the exposé was the reaction of Baker who represented the archetype muckraker and full-fledged progressive.

The common ritual for a muckraker was to heighten and color the particular abuses he found and then suggest effective legislation to curb them. Baker, in a matter-of-fact tone, itemized the endless list of cruel abuses handed the Negro; but he counseled that time, education, and the South formed the holy trinity of Negro salvation. He ridiculed those who "seek to do quickly by medication what can only be accomplished by deliberate hygiene."[27]

North or south of the Mason-Dixon line, Baker found little difference in the attitude of whites toward Negroes. He discovered that a small percentage of the older people in the North still retained some of the Civil War sentiment for the Negro; but generally, most people did not care about or want to discuss him. The pervasive attitude in the North was: "We have helped the Negro to liberty; we have helped to educate him; we have encouraged him to stand on his own feet. Now let's see what he can do for himself."[28] Baker disclosed that he was astounded by the rapidity with which northerners who go South adopt the "southern point of view" on race relations; but, he wrote,

". . . it is the doctrine which many of them, down in their hearts, really believe."[29]

In the South he found the Negro living in utter terror. He told how a young, good-looking Negro walking down the sidewalk accidentally bumped into a white woman. When the young man discovered whom he had bumped, his face reflected abject horror and he raced off wildly down the alley. The Negro, Baker claimed, knew that if the woman accused him of insult or attack, he would soon be the subject of a white lynch mob.[30]

While in Georgia, Baker learned the inside story of the Atlanta race riot of 1906. He found that in connection with Hoke Smith's campaign for governor, Negro-baiting politicians and newspapermen had aggravated racial tension until Atlanta was engulfed in a wave of "primordial savagery." Just before the riot, the Atlanta *News* had printed five extra editions saturated with descriptions of brazen atrocities committed by Negroes. On September 22, the second-edition headlines of the Atlanta *Journal* read: "ANGRY CITIZENS IN PURSUIT OF BLACK BRUTE WHO ATTEMPTED ASSAULT . . . MRS. CHAPIN RESCUED FROM FIEND BY PASSING NEIGHBOR."[31] Bombarded by a sensational press and a white-supremacy campaign, Atlanta needed but a trivial incident to ignite a race riot that drenched the city with Negro blood.

Examining the Jim Crow system, Baker observed that segregation allowed only the worst elements of the races to come in contact, while their best elements had virtually no social intercourse. Still he approved of segregation as the only practical means for the peculiar southern situation.[32] Echoing Booker Washington, Baker advised the Negro to stay out of politics and seek to better his situation in more practical ways. He confided that, rightly or wrongly, the North had approved of disfranchisement. Besides, he added, the Fifteenth Amendment could not enfranchise the Negro. "Men," Baker declared, "must enfranchise themselves."[33]

Concerning education, Baker discovered that the South was adamant about educating Negroes. The South loved the "mammies and uncles," persons who would "do their duty and not fuss about it." It was the intelligent and educated Negro that southerners disliked and distrusted.[34] Baker explained lynching not in terms of race hatred, but in terms of the southerner's distrust of judicial proceedings. Anyway, he concluded: "The South is making fully as good progress in overcoming its peculiar forms of lawlessness as the North is. . . ."[35]

In light of his findings, Baker's conclusions were striking indeed. His answer to the race problem did not stir a bristle on the touchy southerner. To be sure, Baker reported that the Negro suffered every conceivable discrimination in labor, in the courts, and at the polls. The colored man lived in an atmosphere of sudden terror. The intelligent and ambitious Negro was the subject of southern animosity. Nevertheless, Baker surmised that the white man "with his higher cultivation, his keener sensibilities, his memories of departed glory had suffered far more."[36] Apparently, Baker thought that both black and white were victimized by the irrevocable past—the one because of inferior heredity and the incubus of slavery, the other because of a high civilization accompanied by undue pride and a stuffy culture. Baker's final word was to let social relationships alone, for ". . . the less they are talked about the better." Optimistically, he predicted that the South would rear a new leadership of "constructive ability and unselfish patriotism" which would turn away from the timeworn Negro issue.[37] How strange it seems that a muckraking progressive would equate "constructive" leadership with evasion of the Negro problem. Perhaps he dreamed that the Negro would accept forever his degrading peonage in the land of opportunity and that the whole sticky situation would painlessly evaporate. Certainly Ray Stannard Baker exemplified his theory that a northerner gone South soon adopted the "southern point of view on the race issue."

42

Baker was not atypical of the progressive journalist or the progressive press in its entirety. If the liberal press was not cool to Negro rights, it was quite often hostile. Under the editorship of Lyman Abbott, it was clear that the influential *Outlook* would not take up the cause of Negro justice. Other progressive magazines such as *McClure's* and *The Arena*, usually energetic exposers of social injustices, were only slightly concerned with the Negro problem. The fact was that many of the articles on Negroes in these two candid magazines were written by southerners or persons with staunchly anti-Negro views.

In *McClure's* short time of glory, Thomas Nelson Page, a romantic novelist and arrogant white supremacist who idealized the old South, wrote the most prominent articles pertaining to the Negro. In unvarnished language, Page depicted the Negro as inferior, oversexed, and morally depraved. Equality meant but one thing to a young Negro, Page claimed: the right to share a bed with a white woman.[38] In a representative article in *The Arena*, a Massachusetts author implored his colleagues: "Enough of fanaticism and mawkish sentimentalism; . . . Race prejudice is in a large sense beneficent, in that it has kept the negro race remarkably pure."[39]

Racism was the ascendant theme when the progressive press discussed Negroes. The innate inferiority of the Negro was always clearly professed, although a feeling of paternalism and responsibility for the Negro was sometimes voiced. An article in the *Atlantic Monthly* by an author claiming to be of neither southern nor northern sentiment but wholly impartial, expressed no doubt of Negro inferiority. The Negro, he wrote, should not be elevated "above his proper sphere"; but whites should recognize his inalienable rights. Though a lesser breed, the Negro should not be degraded to the level of a brute animal.[40]

The liberal magazines praised the Negro's easy acceptance of servility, and they frowned upon any pretense of Negro equality. "His dream of social and political equality is passing . . .

43

and the white man and the black are dwelling together in harmony," accepting the fact that God made one the ruler and one the ruled, went an article in *The Arena*. "To say that the blacks are the equals of the whites, mentally, morally, or physically," continued the New Yorker, "is a libel on the Anglo-Saxon race."[41] The slightest betterment of the Negro brought condemnation if it entailed the disturbing of blissful tranquillity. When President Roosevelt appointed a Negro to the Collectorship of the Port of Charleston, South Carolina, the *American Review of Reviews* scolded that had the appointee been interested in the welfare of his race, he would have tactfully refused the position.[42]

Evidently, northerners more than southerners still contemplated the colonization of the unwanted blacks. "Any Congressman should deem it the most useful and honorable act of his life," one article in *The Arena* said, "to vote a hundred millions of Federal cash to . . . transport to Cuba all the surplus and threatening blacks of the South."[43] The *Outlook* nodded to the school of thought which held that the Negro was a born vagrant, sex fiend, and criminal. "There is no doubt," wrote the editors, "that negroes are continually guilty of brutal assaults upon white women, and that among negroes there is widespread indolence and shiftlessness." An article in the *Forum*, another mouthpiece of progressive ideas, purported that the Negro was "morally relaxative." The author asserted that the "rag-time music" (jazz) of the Negro was symbolic of his primitive morality. "How could it be different," he asked, "when the music had its birth through the sensuously sonorous larynx of the negro and was first voiced from his sensuously formed mouth."[44] Apparently obsessed with Negro sexual prowess, the author warned that the sexual seductiveness of the barbarous, pagan black would destroy Anglo-Saxon civilization. Seldom could superior races resist the sexual attractiveness of a lower race. After all, he stated, "Marc Anthony [*sic*] is not the only instance—and it is said that Cleopatra was an Ethiop."[45]

44

On the question of disfranchisement, the progressive press concurred with southern sentiment and explanations. James Boyle, a professor at the University of Wisconsin, commented in *The Arena*: "They gave the members of the inferior race a fair trial, and then disfranchised them. They were found unfit, even after years of freedom to participate in the administration of the high functions of a republican form of government."[46] The *American Review of Reviews* gave only passing notice to the suffrage controversy. "The great fact is that, theoretically, every negro in the South is perfectly entitled to vote and hold office," it declared. "He is merely asked to comply with certain reasonable conditions."[47] *The World's Work* asked that the South disfranchise "without doing violence" to the Constitution; then the North would not be greatly concerned.[48] The *Outlook* added that Force Bills and federal marshals were not to be used to force the North's "ideal of brotherhood" on the South.[49]

Seemingly, it never occurred to the egalitarian progressives that disfranchisement of a race might be considered undemocratic. The only ground on which progressives ever contested Negro disfranchisement was that it caused unequal representation of voters in the Congress. Edward Atkinson perceived that although the Negroes had been disfranchised, they were still represented in the federal Congress. So, in a sense, the North was being disfranchised in the Congress by the disfranchisement of Negroes in the South.[50] In *Following the Color Line*, Baker revealed that in 1902 South Carolinians cast only 4,600 votes for each congressman, while New Yorkers cast over 40,000 votes for each representative.[51] In effect, a small minority of the nation's voters in the South wielded influence in Congress far out of proportion to its numbers. Moreover, the Fourteenth Amendment explicitly demanded that Congressional representation must be reduced when persons were disfranchised for reasons other than treason or criminality. However, no attempt was made to enforce the law of the land.

An indifferent North no longer became excited about tales of Negro lynchings. A correspondent who had just covered the lynching of six Negroes in Florida complained that press associations would not carry lynching news any more. Editorial comment on such happenings, he wrote, had become a rarity.[52]

Besides journalistic opinion, science—or near-science— placed its stamp of approval on racist theories. An article by a medical doctor in *The Century Magazine* (New York) conformed especially well to the orthodox liturgy of racism. Dr. Robert Bennett Bean of Johns Hopkins University, after a lengthy study of the human brain, proclaimed that the Negro brain was smaller than the Caucasian brain. "Due to the deficiency of gray matter in the negro brain," Dr. Bean concluded that it was futile to try educating the Negro. The Caucasian and the Negro were at the extreme and opposite ends of evolution. Because of his brain makeup, the Negro was "affectionate, immensely emotional, sensual, and under provocation, passionate." Also the Negro had a singular lack of judgment.[53] Besides the medical profession, sociologists, psychologists, and anthropologists added considerable impetus to American racism.[54]

Somewhat paradoxically, a press that was convinced of Negro inferiority was quick to announce that the Negro had made significant gains in the face of overwhelming odds. A favorite pastime of progressive editors was to compare the status of American Negroes with other backward peoples of the world —a kind of comparative poverty. Perhaps only by comparison could a progressive soothe his reform-minded conscience. In 1913, on the fiftieth anniversary of Negro freedom, *The World's Work* reported that in a half century the American Negro had advanced much farther economically than the Russian serfs who were freed in 1861. Since emancipation, the Russian serf had accumulated an average of thirty-six dollars in property. On the other hand, the Negro had acquired seventy dollars' worth of property per capita.[55] The editors, of course, did not foresee that

46

the Russian peasants four years hence would participate in a bloody revolution. The common feeling was that the American Negro was well off, especially when compared to his African brothers. Politically and socially, he was happier in the United States than anywhere else in the world.[56]

Basically, the progressive press accepted as fact the theory of Negro inferiority and the corollary of Negro criminality and indolence. Complete assimilation of the Negro into American life was impossible; since the Negro was what he was, whites must be left free to cope with him as the situation required— even if that meant undemocratic and violent means.

On a slightly higher plateau of theorizing than the muck-raking magazines were the works of liberal intellectuals who were often in the forefront of the progressive movement. On the whole, however, the attitude of the intellectuals toward the Negro was very similar to that of the liberal magazines. For one thing, the intellectuals of the progressive movement were gravely influenced by professors who were proponents of the Teutonic-origins theory—a theory which maintained that only Teutonic peoples were fit to govern. Professor John W. Burgess of Columbia University, one of the foremost advocates of this theory, boasted of the virtual control of American universities by men of his thinking.[57] In his thirty-six years of teaching political science at Columbia, Burgess's star pupil was Theodore Roosevelt; he considered Roosevelt and Kaiser Wilhelm to be the two greatest living men of their time. Herbert Baxter Adams, who organized the Johns Hopkins Graduate School, was also an adherent to the theory of Teutonic superiority. One of his best students was a young idealist named Woodrow Wilson.

Pupils of Burgess, Adams, and other Teutonic-supremacist professors[58] ingeniously twisted the race theories of their teachers to suit their psychological needs. Those of English ancestry substituted Anglo-Saxon supremacy for the Teutonic variety. Theodore Roosevelt, a descendant of Dutch settlers, did not

47

quite fit either category, so he conveniently created the "American race" and gave it superior qualities. In the main, the ideas about race emanating from the universities seemed like ardent and labored sophistry.

Exemplifying the racial ideas of a young intellectual were those of Frederic C. Howe, expressed in his memoirs. A pupil of Woodrow Wilson at Johns Hopkins, Howe felt that his education placed upon him responsibility and a mission to better the world. Yet his announcement of a calling for service seemed rather forced. "I had a hazy sense of the brotherhood of man, but was not greatly moved by it," he confessed. "I liked my own kind of people . . . who read books and talked about them. I had a strong belief in the superiority of the Anglo-Saxon." His conclusion was that the English-speaking people were the chosen ones to carry on progressive civilization.[59] Howe went on to become one of the most effective city planners and reformers in the Progressive era.

Besides the Teutonic-origins theory and all of its ramifications, there were also the forces of Charles Darwin and Herbert Spencer at work in the American universities. These, too, had racist connotations. Darwin originated the theory of biological evolution, and Spencer (1820-1903) gave Darwinism a social form and substance. Spencer, for instance, coined the well-known phrases "survival of the fittest" and the "struggle for existence."[60] Spencer maintained that government should remain aloof from the struggle of society. Incessant struggle, even war, was necessary to eliminate inferior beings so that progress could take place. As industrialism overtook the nation, economics was to be the main arena of struggle. With such a philosophy, business magnates lionized Spencer. When Andrew Carnegie read Spencer's works, he confided that "light came as in a flood and all was clear."[61]

Spencer's leading American disciple was William Graham Sumner, professor of political science at Yale. Sumner maintained that there should be no ethical or governmental interference in the struggle of the races. His favorite refrain was: "Stateways cannot change folkways." On the race problem his naturalistic outlook was that "the results will be such as the facts and forces call for." Never did they depend on an ethical element.[62] A man, he declared, could do no more than curse his fate were he born to an inferior race.[63]

Around the beginning of the twentieth century, a number of progressive intellectuals began to challenge effectively the social Darwinism of Spencer and Sumner. The scholarly liberals denied that society or economic enterprise should be a vicious struggle for existence, and they denounced the negative and amoral view of government espoused by Darwinist conservatives. Still the very same progressives most inconsistently lauded the "struggle of the races," and concluded that an inferior race like the Negro deserved no better than second-class citizenship. For instance, Edward A. Ross of the University of Wisconsin was a commanding figure who vehemently opposed the philosophy of *laissez-faire* and biological determinism. Ross branded the religion of *laissez-faire* as nothing but a vile corruption of Darwinism. A devout democrat, Ross was a friend of the Populists and the muckrakers.[64] He lent a hand to La Follette in his crusade to reform the state of Wisconsin. In addition, his twenty-four books on sociology and politics did much to counter the philosophy of the Sumner school.

Ross was primarily concerned with labor unions, which he felt were a necessity to combat the evils of industrialism. Since immigration flooded the labor market and neutralized the work of labor leaders, Ross joined most of his northern colleagues in denouncing immigration. However, Ross did not base his anti-immigration arguments on practical terms as an enlightened progressive might have; but he conjured up the old bogey of racism. While discarding Spencer's biological analogies to politics and society, Ross did not hesitate to employ them freely in his defense of racism. In *The Old World in the New* Ross stigmatized all the "new immigrants" as "strikebreakers and scabs" from lower races. They were alcoholics, unhygienic, and prone to illiteracy and insanity.[65] He cried out against the millions of inferior immigrants who were lowering the character of America. A nation must have "pride of blood" and an "uncompromising attitude toward lower races," he declared. As might be expected, Ross employed his racist arguments against the ill-bred Negro.[66]

John R. Commons was another progressive whose racial ideas seemed awkwardly at variance with his democratic theories. Like Ross, Commons was a professor at the University of Wisconsin and a member of La Follette's brain trust. Often more of a doer than a theorizer, he drafted a new civil-service law for La Follette, helped reorganize the municipal government of Milwaukee, and served as a revered adviser on labor issues.[67] In his originality and liberalism, Commons was truly representative of the Progressive era.[68]

Nevertheless, on matters pertaining to race, Commons seemed more of a reactor than a thinker. As with Ross, his racism was connected with his opposition to immigration; but in his harangues against immigrants he did not fail to chastise the Negro race. In *Races and Immigrants* (1907), Commons wrote that all tropical races were "indolent and fickle." The only way that a Negro would adopt the strenuous life of the Anglo-Saxon, he said, was by some kind of coercion. Moreover, the Negro was "lacking in the mechanical idea" so necessary for an advanced industrial society.[69]

Still another liberal in the intellectual world who had an explicit Negro prejudice was Josiah Royce, professor of philosophy at Harvard. Compared to Ross and Commons, Royce could hardly be called a racist, until he expressed himself on the Negro. He was quite skeptical of the pseudoscientific race theories. He claimed that scientists knew too little about men to

classify them as to their social worth. Royce informed the racists
that at one time in history all men and races had been barbarous.
He demonstrated his rejection of racial theories by illustrating
how the Japanese had advanced in such a short time—their feats
including a military victory over Russia in 1905. The Japanese
example, Royce contended, proved that a race other than Caucasian could attain higher types of wisdom. Before the Chicago
Ethical Society, the erudite professor pleaded for a reexamina-
tion of race psychology: "We all have illusions and hug them.
Let us not sanctify them by the name of science. I am a member
of the human race . . . which is, as a whole, considerably lower
than the angels, so that the whole of it very badly needs race-
elevation."[70]

The doubting Royce was not so unsure of his racial ideas
about the Negro. Here he was ready to leap to a hasty conclusion. He believed that the Negro was a product of a tropical race
with a built-in moral sordidness. The Negro had shown none of
the qualities of the advancing Japanese. The Negro would remain primitive, he concluded, ". . . for reasons which are not
due merely to circumstance but which are quite innate in his
mental constitution."[71] Once again the social optimism of a thor-
oughgoing progressive had been clouded by the presence in
America of millions of nonassimilable Negroes.

Another group that had notable influence in the progressive
movement was the triumvirate of Herbert Croly, Walter Weyl,
and Walter Lippmann. In their published political treatises,
these three supplied the brunt of progressive political theory.
Between 1910 and 1914, Croly, Weyl, and Lippmann were often
guests at Oyster Bay where they enjoyed the hospitality and the
eager ear of Theodore Roosevelt. The *New Republic* (1914),
edited by these three political philosophers, became a bastion of
liberalism in the conservative twenties.

In *The Promise of American Life* Croly was primarily concerned with creating a "national cohesion" of middle-class

51

Americans. He spoke only passingly of the Negro, and then in relationship with the Civil War. Croly assailed both abolitionists and southerners alike for tearing apart the fabric of the nation. He praised Lincoln not for the Emancipation Proclamation but for his farseeing statesmanship in recognizing the sanctity of the Union. As an afterthought, Croly expressed the opinion that southerners were correct in believing that the Negro was morally and intellectually inferior.[72]

In 1914 the precocious Walter Lippmann, just out of Harvard, published his political views in *A Preface to Politics*. Like Croly, Lippmann did not touch directly on the race problem, but did claim that "profound economic forces" had ended chattel slavery. He recognized that emancipation was not in reality freedom for the Negro, for Negro freedom would be a continuing battle subject to changes in the "character and social customs of the nation." The *Preface* was full of Lippmann's newly found Freudianism, Bergsonianism, and Jamesian pragmatism to the point of anti-intellectualism. His political views were devoid of any humanitarian trappings or ethical inclinations. Lippmann's philosophy was: "No creed can possess any final sanction. It is more penetrating . . . to ask any creed whether it served than whether it was true."[73] With such an expedient philosophy, Lippmann was not prone to go off on a crusade for the Negro.

Walter Weyl, however, was not the type to evade the Negro question. In *The New Democracy*, which appeared purposely just before the 1912 election, Weyl, with great soul-searching, took up the perplexing race problem. He commented that the Negro was the most exploited American minority. Racial prejudice had caused the Negro severe industrial handicaps and general disfranchisement. "The South is psychologically cramped," he wrote. "The North is bewildered. The Negro problem is the mortal spot of the new democracy."[74]

Not a real racist in his thinking—he complained against anti-immigration tirades by racists—Weyl still thought that it

was best that democracy lay aside the Negro problem for a
while; but he warned that a prolonged evasion of the problem
might result in a savage race war. On the question of suffrage,
Weyl rationalized that disfranchisement was permissible "if we
can honestly believe that the denial of the Negro vote is advan-
tageous, not only to us, but to him." Considering the Negro vote
in Cincinnati and Philadelphia, he doubted whether it was
worthwhile to secure the Negro vote in Atlanta and Charleston.
Despite his misgivings about the Negro voter, Weyl recom-
mended that the question must ever be open to discussion. "The
mouse," he wrote, "can find many reasons, philanthropic or
other, for not belling the cat."[75]

Being a democrat and a reformer, Weyl visibly struggled
to be generously and consistently liberal in his ideas about the
Negro. Still he could not bring himself to advocate a positive
program to deal with the race problem, even though he recognized the dire portent of denying it. "There may arise a Negro
consciousness, a dark sense of outraged racial dignity. There
may come a stirring of a rebellious spirit among ten, or as it
soon will be, twenty or thirty million black folk." With prophetic insight, Weyl warned that Negroes presently humble
might in the future become "imperious, exigent, and proudly
race-conscious."[76] With those words of wisdom, Weyl went on to
map out the hopeful course of the "new democracy."

The overwhelming fact was that the progressives, for all
their talk of social justice and the brotherhood of man, steered
sharply around the Negro problem. In fact, they considered the
Negro a perpetual lower caste which blighted the "promise of
American life." The apparent failure of reconstruction and the
scientific findings of the time gave credence to the belief that the
Negro race was inferior. Even the old Garrisonians washed their
hands of the Negro. Young intellectuals, subjected to the tutor-
ship of race-conscious professors, interpreted the shortcomings
of the Negro as a result of a forever unalterable and benighted

heritage. No social scientists sought to explain that the Negro had a legion of millstones around his social, political, and economic neck, dragging him down to the grisly depths of servility. In sum, the bulk of the northern progressives, either candidly or clandestinely, wore the garb of racism just as surely as did the southern white supremacists.

From 1901 to 1914, *progress* was the sacrosanct word on the tip of the liberal tongue. The motivation for this quest for progress, however, was the "pride of blood"—in essence, the manifest destiny of Anglo-Saxonism. The pervasive feeling of tough-minded progressives was that the "lower races" had no rights that infallible progress was bound to respect. This powerful magnetic current combining progress and Anglo-Saxonism raced along almost unchallenged. Only a few of the adventurously independent and pure, who felt their strength tenfold, dared resist the double-barreled current. These lonely pilgrims were the humanitarian progressives or the new abolitionists.

HUMANITARIAN PROGRESSIVES—

THE RISE

OF THE NEW ABOLITIONISTS

The ever-diminishing political and social status of Negroes and the wholesale violence perpetrated upon them triggered a revolt among northern Negro intellectuals. Denouncing the submissive leadership of Booker Washington, these Negro rebels promised to agitate until they received every right belonging to them as Americans. The Negro revolt soon found enthusiastic support from a group of idealistic and humanitarian whites who had come to feel that Negroes must demand and get the full rights promised them under the Constitution. This unpopular and infinitesimal minority of reformers—the new abolitionists —though subjected to rancorous and sustained vilification from the thriving multitudes of racists, wrote a saga of herculean courage and extraordinary persistence. In the face of stultifying odds, this small group began an arduous climb that ultimately carried them to a height where they became a conspicuous and powerful directing force in the parade of American events.

The leader of the Negro revolt was W. E. B. DuBois, an erudite scholar and intellectual who was the first Negro to receive a doctorate from Harvard. DuBois was born a free Negro in Great Barrington, Massachusetts, as he put it, "with a flood of Negro blood, a strain of French, a bit of Dutch, but thank God! no 'Anglo-Saxon.' "[1] A man of high culture and keen perception, DuBois was acutely sensitive to discrimination shown to Negroes; and he released his pent-up emotions in a fiery competitiveness with the whole Caucasian race. In a book of sketches entitled *The Souls of Black Folk* (1903), DuBois expressed, possibly better than any other Negro of his time, "the strange meaning of being black" at the beginning of the twentieth century. Plaintively he related how during elementary school he had suddenly discovered that he was different when a newly arrived girl "peremptorily, without a glance" refused his greeting card. From then on DuBois ever felt his "two-ness—an American, a Negro; two souls, two thoughts, two unreconciled strivings; two warring ideals in one dark body. . . ." DuBois resolved to take revenge on the pale world about him by surpassing whites in all things. His greatest joy, he explained, was to best white students at examination time, or to beat them in a foot race, or simply "to beat their stringy heads."[2]

Temperamentally and philosophically, DuBois and Booker Washington differed as day and night. Washington was like a father to the Negro race, DuBois like a gadfly. Washington stressed agricultural and industrial training as implements to improve the Negroes' status. DuBois stressed higher education, declaring that only "exceptional men" from the "Talented Tenth" could rescue the foundering Negro. He scoffed at the

56

idea that lowly Negro workmen, taking jobs that white men scorned, would win the respect of belligerent whites. DuBois accused Washington of designing "a voteless herd to run the machines and wash the dishes for the new aristocracy."[3] How, he asked, could a people "deprived of political rights, made a servile caste, and allowed only the most meagre chance for developing their exceptional men" make effective progress in society along economic lines?[4]

In 1905 DuBois and a small group of Negro intellectuals who chafed under Booker Washington's easygoing leadership started a movement of their own. At Niagara Falls, Canada— they met here because of discrimination in a hotel on the American side—these militant Negroes drafted a resolution of historic importance: "We claim for ourselves every single right that belongs to a freeborn American, political, civil, and social, and until we get these rights, we will never cease to protest and assail the ears of America."[5] There was no mistaking language of such a concise and inspired nature. The militant civil-rights movement of the twentieth century had begun.

The group met a few times more, once on the historic site of Harper's Ferry, where some of the Negroes walked barefoot over John Brown's path. Public opinion predictably branded the Niagara movement radical, and it died in the bud.[6] But in 1909 a movement of much greater duration emerged and adopted the Niagara platform and most of its advocates. The new organization was to become known under the heading of NAACP, the National Association for the Advancement of Colored People.

The immediate event that led to the formation of the NAACP was a sanguinary race riot in Springfield, Illinois, in August 1908. For two gory days chaos reigned before the state militia restored order. William English Walling, an able journalist of independent means, a compulsive reformer, and a sometime socialist, hurried from Chicago to report the riot.[7] He found that a white mob had lynched and mutilated Negroes in

57

the very shadow of Abraham Lincoln's home. In a kind of Anglo-Saxon passover the mob burned virtually all the Negro housing of Springfield. White handkerchiefs were fastened to houses owned by whites, and residences lacking this "seal of good housekeeping" were put to the torch. As the white mob rampaged and wantonly pillaged, they shouted: "Lincoln freed you, we'll show you where you belong."[8]

Walling and his wife, having just spent two years in Tsarist Russia studying the 1905 revolution, had been extremely relieved to reenter free America. But Walling announced that the explosive race hatred in Springfield was worse than the Russian's hatred of the Jew. In Russia the Tsar deliberately precipitated pogroms, but in America such outrages were spontaneous and unashamed.[9] Walling found that whites were boastful of murder and plunder. Kate Howard, an elephantine rowdy who incited the riot, proudly exhibited buckshot wounds in her fleshy arms, wounds which a brave Negro defending his home had inflicted. The mob, according to the white law of retributive justice, lynched and mangled the Negro. When Walling interviewed many of the still-carousing whites, they exclaimed: "Why the niggers came to think they were as good as we are." The *Illinois State Journal*, a Springfield newspaper, as well as four leading ministers of the town demanded "swift justice" for the criminal Negro, whose "general inferiority" and "unfitness for free institutions" were causing the city's ills. Actually, the spark that had set off the riot was the accusation, perhaps false, that a Negro had raped a white woman.[10] The mere charge of a Negro with a serious crime was enough to bring the white man's wrath down upon all Negroes, innocent included.

Walling sensed that the gravity of the problem of race friction in the United States demanded a drastic solution. "Either the spirit of Lincoln and Lovejoy must be revived and we must come to treat the Negro on a plane of absolute political and social equality," he wrote; "or Vardaman and Tillman will soon

58

have transferred the race war to the North." Concluding the article, Walling challenged the nation by asking what group of Americans would consider the seriousness of the problem and come to the aid of the Negro.[11]

The poignancy of Walling's article aroused Mary White Ovington, a white social worker who had been studying the Negro problem in New York City. Conferring with Walling, she decided to enlist Oswald Garrison Villard, the influential editor of the New York *Evening Post*, to form an organization devoted to securing Negro justice. In Villard she picked a man admirably suited and equal to the task. Enjoying the dubious distinction of being the grandson of William Lloyd Garrison, Villard was a highly competent, independent, and honest journalist with a verve for reform.[12] In 1902 Villard referred to himself as "a young radical none too tactful, and ready to believe that truths which shocked were sometimes called for."[13] Reinforced with such daring resolve, Villard threw himself wholeheartedly into the battle for Negro rights.

Villard's initial strategy was to draw up a strong statement on Negro rights and circulate it to be signed by prominent, reform-minded people. For publicity purposes, the statement, the "Call," was to be announced on February 12, 1909, the centenary of Lincoln's birth.[14] Coming from Villard's facile pen, the "Call" was a powerfully worded and impressive document. It stated that if Lincoln were to visit twentieth-century America, he would be startled to see that whites and Negroes "could not frequent the same market place." This nation, it read, could exist half free and half slave no better in 1909 than in 1861. Hence, Villard concluded, "We call upon all believers in democracy to join in a national conference for the discussion of present evils, the voicing of protests, and the renewal of the struggle for civil and political liberty."[15]

A small but distinguished group of Americans undersigned the "Call." Among the notables who signed were Jane Addams,

John Dewey, William Dean Howells, Lincoln Steffens, Clarence Darrow, and W. E. B. DuBois. Once again organized abolition had raised its emotional and controversial head.

The publicity that Villard sought by announcing on Lincoln's birthday the invitation for a national conference on Negro rights did not materialize. The New York *Times* gave only the briefest notice of the newly born civil-rights movement. On the other hand, the attendance of Booker Washington at the annual Lincoln Dinner of the Republican Club in the Waldorf-Astoria got abundant and stilted print. The differing flavor of the speech which Washington delivered that night and the "Call" which Villard produced seemed incredible. "Like Lincoln," Washington said, "the negro race should seek to be simple. . . . We . . . should, like Lincoln, have moral courage to be what we are and not pretend to be what we are not."[16] The *Times* portrayed Washington as a man of "lofty ideals" and "penetrating intelligence," who had "a profound and catholic conception of life." If happy fatalism was "lofty" idealism, and obeisance before the mighty Anglo-Saxon was a "catholic conception of life," then the *Times* had accurately described Washington. Whatever the merit of his philosophy, Washington, to be sure, was infinitely popular.[17]

Somewhat ironically, February 12, 1909, was also the centennial of Charles Darwin's birth. Only a few columns away from the *Times'* eulogy of Washington was a laudatory appraisal of the great biological emancipator. The *Times* perhaps felt that it was appropriate to delineate the sociological ideals of the venerable Washington and the naturalistic theory of Charles Darwin in cozy proximity.[18]

In 1910, after the trial balloon sent up on Lincoln's birthday, Villard and other white leaders officially incorporated the NAACP. At its inception the NAACP was primarily a white organization, the only Negro officer being DuBois. As director of publicity and research, DuBois nevertheless became the eyes, ears, and the mouth of the new organization. He marshaled all of his skill to release a reservoir of dammed-up invective in publishing the *Crisis*, the official mouthpiece of the NAACP. In a short time the *Crisis* was enjoying a substantial circulation.[19] At last, the Negro had a reliable and powerful amplifier with which to accost the ears of America.

In addition to Walling, Villard, and DuBois, there were other astute and prestigious men and women who rendered service to the cause of Negro justice. Moorfield Storey, the first president of the NAACP, was one of these. Storey was born of a family long entrenched in high Bostonian society. Having served as Charles Sumner's secretary from 1867 to 1869, he had strong abolitionist roots. A Harvard graduate, an esteemed lawyer, and an author—he wrote Charles Sumner's biography— Storey was one of those rare political independents and idealists who made heroic efforts to apply abstract principles of justice to problematic reality.[20] By doing so, he became a perpetual espouser of noble but unpopular causes.

Storey spent a large part of his life agitating for equal rights for all people living under the American flag. This habit first led him on a crusade against imperialism in the Philippines —he was president of the Anti-Imperialist League—and then on a campaign for Philippine independence. Failing in these endeavors, he turned to the cause of Negro rights.[21] Storey maintained that American policy in regard to the Negro had been disastrous, and the inevitable antidote was another antislavery crusade. In substantiation of his race views, he was fond of quoting Lincoln: "They who deny freedom to others deserve it not themselves, and under a just God will not long retain it."[22]

Storey believed that the potential of the Negro was equal to that of the white. In fact, he declared that race tension was largely caused by the ability of the Negro to rise in American civilization. Not just content to sit on the sidelines and theorize, Storey performed valuable services for the Negro. He exercised his legal ability and his prestige as former president of the American Bar to assist in the few Negro victories handed down by the conservative courts. In 1915, primarily because of Storey's legal finesse, the Supreme Court invalidated the "grandfather clause."[23]

Following in the humanitarian steps of Storey, Jane Addams of Hull House fame was another tireless worker for Negro rights. In fact, she crusaded for a variety of human rights, whether for Indian, immigrant, or unwed mother. In 1913 she declared in *The Survey* that all of the political tranquillity and prosperity of the day had been built on the work of a previous generation of reformers. But the present generation, she contended, was content simply to nod in recognition and deny the strenuous task of completing unfinished reforms. "How far," she asked, "are we responsible that their [Negro] civil rights are often rendered futile . . . ? How far has the act of the great emancipator been nullified by our own national indifference?" Miss Addams proclaimed that it was time that America decided whether the old abolitionist arguments were "flat and stale" and whether there was any remaining inclination "to remove fetters, to prevent cruelty," and to beckon "the humblest to the banquet of civilization."[24]

The liberal press was, true to form, primarily hostile to the sentiments of such as Storey and Jane Addams. The festering Negro question was kept in the background as much as possible. After 1910, however, the Negro had DuBois' *Crisis* and also Villard's *Evening Post*, one of the few influential dailies always friendly to the black man.

Among the muckraking sheets, the only progressive magazine that did not equivocate, did not excuse, and did not retreat a single inch on Negro rights was the *Independent*. William Hayes Ward, the editor of the *Independent* from 1896 to 1913, was a brilliant classical and Oriental scholar who turned down a chair at Harvard to become a journalist.[25] As a journalist,

Ward had a hungry passion for righteousness in the civic life of the nation. Under his editorship, the *Independent* was much maligned for its championing of the Negro. In 1912 Ward and his assistant editors endeavored to answer critics by explaining why they were so concerned with Negro rights. First the *Independent* pointed out that Negroes comprised one ninth of the American population, and they were by far the "worst opprest" group in the nation. Therefore, it declared, progressives should throw aside lesser injustices until the Negro was redeemed. "Do you ever hear of any attempt to prevent other citizens from voting or even the proposition to exclude them from the ballot?" queried the *Independent*.[26]

The editors of the *Independent* argued too that Negro suffrage was necessary in order to raise the educational and economic level of the colored people. If Negroes had the ballot, they maintained, then intelligent people would see that they were educated. For instance, the editors divulged, the education of the common people in England followed, not preceded, the ballot.[27] The *Independent* also claimed that the Republican party needed to conciliate the Negroes of the Niagara-movement type, not just the meek followers of Booker Washington. The editors added that any attempt to reduce Congressional representation of the South because of Negro disfranchisement would be a stark evasion of the race problem. In effect, the *Independent* declared, it would be a permanent acceptance of Negro disfranchisement by the national government.[28]

More than just campaigning for Negro suffrage and social equality, agitators for Negro rights began to answer defiantly the racist charges of Negro inferiority, criminality, and immorality. They blamed a pernicious environment and a history of white oppression for Negro failures. Kelly Miller, a Negro educator from Howard University, sharply answered critics who berated blacks for not rising to the top with the cream of civilization. Miller asked how Negroes could be expected to produce

63

a Napoleon when forbidden to carry arms; or how they could be great scholars when only a few years ago they were denied the use of letters; or how they could groom a great statesman when the black man could not vote.[29]

In answer to Negro indictments, DuBois also was a master of devastating repartee. To charges of Negro crime, he retorted that slavery and lynching were the arch crimes. To what the South saw as the worst Negro offense, rape, he replied: "The rape which your gentlemen have done against helpless black women in defiance of your own laws is written on the foreheads of two million mulattoes, and written in ineffaceable blood."[30]

In addition to colored leaders such as Kelly Miller and W. E. B. DuBois, some notable whites came to the defense of the colored race. Henry George, the white social and political philosopher of single-tax fame, also disclaimed charges of Negro inferiority. His long and varied social experiences had converted him from a belief in the supremacy of the white race *per se*. George observed that Negro children learned as rapidly as the white; but, he explained, as soon as the Negroes got old enough to realize that they were considered an inferior race, fated for all time to be cooks and waiters, they lost their ambition. In modern-sounding logic, George asserted: "The influence of heredity . . . is as nothing compared with influences which mold the man after he comes into the world."[31]

Clarence Darrow, a highly touted lawyer and incessant liberal, also belittled arguments of Negro inferiority. Darrow relished the job of defending underdogs—even monkeys.[32] He contemptuously jeered at those who wallowed in Anglo-Saxon race pride. He once remarked that Anglo-Saxons were "the greatest race of sons of bitches that ever infested the earth." And "mind you," he added, "if there is such a race, I am one of them. . . . But I do not brag about it; I apologize for it."[33]

In addition to his penchant for damning his race, Darrow had what were considered radical theories of human behavior.

64

Like Henry George, he placed emphasis on environmental factors regarding human actions. "There is no such thing as crime as the word is generally understood," he explained; for "if every man, woman, and child in the world had a chance to make a decent, fair, honest living, there would be no jails and no lawyers and no courts."[34] Darrow applied his liberal views in defending the Negro who was charged, not falsely, with a high crime rate. He perceived as time went on that the lordly Anglo-Saxon was beginning to worry about this "environment business." "Asking how people grew up," he chuckled, "may make all men equal yet."[35]

William Walling, writing in the *Independent* a year after the Springfield riot, challenged the racist theories of scientists and pseudoscientists, which, he declared, were destroying the feeling of brotherhood among the youth. "When few people . . . are showing greater physiological advance than those of the United States, the most mixed race of all," he marveled, "the age-old argument for 'pure blood' is actually finding scientific support among us!" Walling, in fact, suggested that the mixing of the races had been largely responsible for the advance of civilization.[36] It was the incestuous royal families, he claimed, that produced deformed and eccentric specimens of humanity.

The voices of such able defenders of Negro rights as Walling, Villard, DuBois, and Jane Addams were barely audible above the gale of racism. Yet this small group tried valiantly to apply progressive principles of democracy to all people. In 1912, when William Allen White wrote that progressivism was a great idealistic movement "guided by a passion for humanity," he had accurately described only this small branch of progressives who pledged themselves to destroy the color line in American life.[37] Being the minority that they were, this group of humanitarian progressives experienced chronic failures in their lofty objectives. In 1911 at Boston, Villard, speaking in support of the NAACP, described with great foreboding the sentiment of the nation: "There can be no doubt that a wave of color hysteria is sweeping over the country."[38]

Still, in the face of deafening opposition, leaders of DuBois' and Villard's caliber established a foothold for the Negro rights movement that it never relinquished. They continued to "assail the ears of America," even though few listened. The supreme effort of the new abolitionists, however, was to get the Negro question back into national politics—that mercurial and convulsive but ever decisive arena of give and take where over three million black slaves had found their freedom.

SQUARE DEAL TO NEW FREEDOM—

WHITES ONLY!

Historians have usually attributed to Theodore Roosevelt far greater sympathy for the Negro than he actually possessed.[1] They have sung praises to him for bravely withstanding the storm of southern indignation over the Booker Washington dinner and for making subsequent appointments of certain Negroes to federal office. Roosevelt's initial sound and fury in behalf of the Negro, however, signified nothing—at least nothing more than political expediency. Indeed, the former Rough Rider accepted uncritically the doctrine of white supremacy. In a 1906 letter to Owen Wister, a writer who had just completed a novel with strong racist overtones, Roosevelt candidly wrote:

"Now as to the negroes! I entirely agree with you that as a race they . . . are altogether inferior to the whites."[2] It is not astounding, therefore, that Roosevelt's Square Deal cut corners when applied to Negroes.

In 1912, when Woodrow Wilson's New Freedom triumphed over Roosevelt and Taft, a southerner for the first time since 1848 became president. Wilson's presidency ushered in a new and unprecedented phase of racism and discrimination against colored people in America. At the twilight of the Progressive era, the American Negro had reached the nadir of his political existence. Every conceivable political door approached by the colored man in the fervent period of progressivism was coldly closed in his face. In the summer of 1913, Booker Washington, a man given to chronic understatements about his race, wrote to Oswald Villard: "I have recently spent several days in Washington, and I have never seen the colored people so discouraged and bitter as they are at the present time."[3]

Ironically, an era that ended so despairingly for the Negro had begun with great promise. Back in 1901, Roosevelt's advent to the presidency had aroused considerable optimism among many Negroes. Soon they began to refer to the young chief executive as "our president."[4] The 1901 visit of Booker Washington to the White House was, of course, a fair omen to the men of color. Then in the following year Roosevelt, seemingly undaunted by the verbal assassination over the Booker Washington dinner, appointed Dr. William D. Crum, a Negro, to the Collectorship of the Port of Charleston, South Carolina. Again the South fulminated against the president's action. A third incident that endeared Roosevelt to the Negroes and led them to believe that they might flourish under the Square Deal was the squabble over a colored postmistress in Indianola, Mississippi. When whites pressured the postmistress—appointed under Benjamin Harrison—to resign, Roosevelt promptly closed the post office in retaliation.[5]

Although many Negroes felt indebted to Roosevelt, his interest in them was strictly *realpolitik*. He invited Washington to the White House to discuss not sociology but political patronage.[6] Roosevelt was looking ahead to the election of 1904, figuring that Mark Hanna, who had dubbed him the "damned cowboy," would be his political opponent. The weak spot in Roosevelt's position was that Hanna controlled the "rotten borough," black Republican delegates in the South.[7] With the advice of Booker Washington, Roosevelt made timely Negro appointments to perform a *coup d'etat* on the Republican machinery of the South.[8] It was no coincidence that Dr. Crum was the top colored Republican leader of the Charleston area. In short, from 1901 to 1904 Roosevelt's policy toward the southern Negro was based on politics, not humanitarianism.

In 1904, after winning the election in his own right, Roosevelt's seemingly altruistic activities in behalf of the Negro abruptly ceased. After 1904 he instead made glaring overtures to reconciliate the white South. He no longer fought "lily-white" Republicanism; in fact, he supported it. Roosevelt's change of attitude was evidenced by the sudden praises of his demeanor by staunch southern racists. In 1905 Thomas Nelson Page reported that the president was "more a democrat than a Republican," a way of saying that he concurred with the chief executive on race relations.[9] William Garrott Brown, an Alabamian who taught history at Yale, congratulated Roosevelt for his "new attitude on the Southern question."[10] Although Roosevelt never recanted publicly his earlier deeds concerning the Negro, in 1906 he secretly confided in a letter to Owen Wister that he had acted unwisely in the Booker Washington incident and the Crum appointment.[11]

A few months after Roosevelt's letter to Wister, some soldiers from a Negro Army battalion stationed near Brownsville, Texas, allegedly "shot up the town," killing one person and wounding two others. Since discovery of the guilty soldiers proved impossible, Roosevelt summarily and dishonorably discharged the whole battalion with no hint of a trial. However, he shrewdly withheld his Brownsville decree until November 9, the day after the Congressional elections. The New York *Herald* declared that if the president had announced his decision before the election, the Republican majority in the House would have diminished from 59 to 14. The New York *Age*, a leading Negro newspaper, called the affair an "outrage upon the rights of citizens who are entitled in civil life to trial by jury and in military life to trial by court martial." Even the usually restrained Booker Washington admitted that this time the president had grievously erred.[12]

The complaints against Roosevelt's action in the Brownsville affair were not unfounded. He dishonorably discharged about 160 men; including veterans of fifteen years' service, six Medal of Honor winners, and thirteen holding certificates for bravery. In addition, these men lost their pensions and were barred from civil-service employment. Roosevelt insisted that the soldiers' guilt was confirmed by "scores of witnesses" and that the whole affair was "a horrible atrocity . . . unparalleled for infamy in the annals of the United States Army."[13]

Senator Joseph B. Foraker of Ohio, undoubtedly motivated by presidential aspirations, challenged Roosevelt on the Brownsville issue. He called Roosevelt's act "illegal, unconstitutional, and unjustifiable."[14] Foraker then called for an investigation into the entire Brownsville matter. Dragging on for several months, the inquiry almost demolished Roosevelt's arguments that the Negro soldiers were guilty beyond doubt. In fact, it tended to exonerate the soldiers and to cause the whole case to appear as a diabolical frame-up by whites who resented the presence of Negroes in Brownsville. Possibly Roosevelt's impulsive action in the affair originated psychologically to serve as atonement for his earlier so-called pampering of the Negro—a deed he had long since regretted.[15] He completely omitted refer-

70

ence to the Brownsville affair in his autobiography. Roosevelt thus spent his second term of office trying to assuage a South which he had alienated by what he now considered a couple of rash acts. At best, he pleaded for southerners not to molest or humiliate what he considered the few exceptional Negroes like Booker Washington. At worst, he was devoid of any statesman-like insight concerning the Negro and his future in America.

As Roosevelt's second term neared its end in 1908, he selected William Howard Taft as his successor; and in November the voters confirmed his choice. While Roosevelt had done little for the Negro in his second term, Taft was to do much less in his four-year tenure. Taft appointed no Negroes to office in the southern states, and he encouraged the establishment of an oligarchic, "lily-white" Republican party in the South.[16] In the election of 1908 Taft did very well in the South for a Republican, and he paid his respects by making a tour there after the election. In one of his southern speeches entitled "The Winning of the South," Taft repeated the precious and irresistible southern idiom that "the best friend of the Negro was the Southern white man." The rotund president also declared that there was nothing inconsistent between the Fourteenth and Fifteenth Amendments and the southern safeguards (disfranchisement) against "domination . . . by an ignorant electorate."[17] Speaking before students at a Negro university in Charlotte, North Carolina, Taft proffered his judgment on the Negro's place in American life. "Your race," he said, pointing at his dusky audience, "is adapted to be a race of farmers first, last, and for all time."[18]

Southerners were heartened by Taft's attitude on color. Walter Hines Page predicted that his southern attitude would break the "solid South."[19] Southern white Republicans availed themselves of the opportunity to fleece the "Black and Tans" of federal patronage. Though Republicans had once gained historical notoriety by using the black man to build their party in the South, they now meticulously excluded him.

71

The Republican party was not alone in its avoidance of the Negro question. The rising Socialist party, often a defender of desperate causes, also performed some nimble philosophical acrobatics to avoid that particular issue. Generally, the Socialists expressed the opinion that the race problem would dissolve along with capitalism. By some magic formula, socialism would automatically end race prejudice. The Socialists made no discernible effort to utilize their party as a vehicle for the betterment of the Negro. On the contrary, a close look at the Socialist movement revealed that it was well tainted with racism.[20]

Eugene V. Debs was one of the few leading Socialists who was sympathetic toward the Negro. He opposed segregation and called for the Negro to abandon his false philosophy of "meekness and humility." When campaigning in the South, Debs refused to speak before segregated audiences. He declared that the Socialist party would "be false to its historical mission" if it denied its own philosophy on account of race considerations. Although Debs outwardly condemned racism, he made no special effort for the Negro within his party. "We have nothing special to offer the Negro," Debs proclaimed; "and we cannot make separate appeals to all races."[21]

Unlike Debs, many Socialists were outright racists. In 1902 Victor Berger, leader of the right faction of the Socialists, stated in his *Socialist Democratic Herald*: "There can be no doubt that the negroes and mulattoes constitute a lower race— that the Caucasian and indeed even the Mongolian have the start on them in civilization by many thousand years."[22] The left and the center of the party explained race prejudice as being caused by deliberate incitement from capitalists who wished to exploit both races. The right more pointedly declared that Negroes were a bunch of degenerates who delighted in raping women and children.[23]

In 1903 the pronounced indifference of the American Socialist party concerning violence to Negroes brought about an inquiry by the International Socialist Bureau. The Socialist party defended itself by saying that American capitalism fostered brutal instincts in whites which led to lynching. Needless to say, the Socialist cure for violence against Negroes was the overthrow of the brutal capitalistic system.[24]

After the Brownsville affair in 1906, the National Committee of the Socialist party voted down a resolution to condemn Roosevelt's action by a vote of 28 to 4, with 25 abstentions.[25] Ignoring Marx's call for all workingmen to unite, the Socialists excluded Negroes from their worldwide proletariat. Ernest Untermann, Socialist candidate for governor of Idaho, boldly asserted that "the question as to what race shall dominate the globe must be met as surely as the question of what class shall own the world."[26] William E. Walling related how a self-professed Socialist swore that he would kill his daughter rather than let her marry a Negro. When Walling replied that he could scarcely be a Socialist with such an inhumanitarian philosophy, the man replied: "Socialism has nothing to do with the brotherhood of man."[27] The crux of the matter was that a political party with a red stigma attached to it was quite hesitant to add a black one to its already heavy load.

Political parties neatly sidestepped the pesky Negro question for a time, but the three-way presidential race of 1912 brought it dramatically to the forefront. The Republican party, which renominated Taft, ceased to give even lip service to Negro rights. For the first time since 1868, the Republicans had no specific plank in their platform making them self-professed champions of Negro rights. Four years earlier the Republican platform had contained an explicit delineation of its historic ties with Negro emancipation; and it had "demanded justice for all men, without regard to race or color." Also the 1908 plank had called for the enforcement, "without reservation," of the Thirteenth, Fourteenth, and Fifteenth Amendments; and it had condemned all "devices" aimed at Negro disfranchisement. In

1912 the words and tone of the previous platform were curiously missing.[28]

Roosevelt, his hat back in the political ring, was the standard-bearer of the new Progressive party. The former president seemed pathetically eager to break the "solid South"—but not with Negro votes. "Really, if I could carry one of the eleven ex-Confederate States," he mused, "I should feel as though I could die happy."[29] Clandestinely, Roosevelt sought to build up a "lily-white" Progressive party in the South, but his plans backfired when four southern states sent two delegations each to the national convention—one black, one white. Forced into a corner, Roosevelt had to make a public stand on the Negro question.

To clarify his position, Roosevelt penned a lengthy letter to Julian Harris, a Georgia Progressive. In this letter, printed in the *Outlook*, he resorted to phrasing that had now become trite among the compromising Progressives; that is, leave the leadership of the southern Progressive party to the "wisest and justest white men" of the South. Only in that way, Roosevelt explained, would the Negro prosper. He pointed out that the Republican party had been under black and corrupt leadership for over forty years and had failed miserably. Therefore, it was the better part of wisdom to try a new plan—a "lily-white" party.[30]

While Roosevelt's letter had been circulating among the Progressives, a fight had been raging in the provisional national committee of the party over the seating of colored delegations from the South. Southern committee members had come to Chicago confident that the Progressive party was a white man's party. Colonel John M. Parker of New Orleans, who acted as Roosevelt's adviser on the South, had warned the ex-president that southerners would not tolerate Negroes in the party. As soon as the chairman ordered the national committee in session, Colonel Parker was on the floor speaking out against Filipino representation in the convention. The Filipinos, like the Negro, he stated, were an "absolute impossibility" in politics. When a fellow Progressive expressed resentment at the Negro analogy, Parker retorted that the Negro question was coming up sooner or later, and it should be settled once and for all.[31]

At Parker's prodding, a special committee took up the question of the contested white and colored delegations from the South. B. F. Fridge, who represented the white Mississippi delegation, admitted that the preamble to the Progressive platform of his state explicitly excluded Negroes. There could be no colored leaders in the party, he stated; for "when you give those people down there a chance to be leaders . . . someone has got to be killed." Senator Joseph M. Dixon of Montana pleaded for the committee to seat the white Florida delegation because an ex-Confederate from that body was going to second the nomination of Roosevelt. Not to seat the white delegation would be the supreme embarrassment to the South and would be interpreted as a Negro victory, he claimed.[32] In the end, the disputed white delegations from Mississippi, Louisiana, and Alabama were seated in favor of the colored. The white Florida delegation was so obviously fraudulent that the committee decided, perhaps as a concession to the Negroes, to seat neither the white nor colored delegates.[33]

It was not surprising that southern committeemen argued so heatedly for a "white man's party," but the exuberant concurrence of northerners was somewhat astounding. Medill McCormick of Illinois, later to become a prominent congressman and senator and most recently the son-in-law of Mark Hanna, expressed agreement that the Progressive party should be purely white. Committeemen from Michigan, Wisconsin, and California made similar white-supremacy stands. E. C. Carrington, Jr., of Maryland warned that if the Negro delegates were seated, the party would lose his state.[34]

The most outspoken northerner on the Negro question was young Matthew Hale of Massachusetts, Phi Beta Kappa at Harvard in 1903 and already a rising lawyer and businessman.

75

Kowtowing before the southerners, he confessed that the fathers and grandfathers of the North had surely been misguided. "Your attitude on the negro problem is right," Hale said, "and ours is wrong." In surrendering, all that Hale begged of his southern colleagues was the same courtesy that Grant gave Lee at Appomattox.[35]

Despite his agreement with the southerners, Hale did have one complaint against them. He felt that the major trouble with southern racists was that they lacked tact—a lack which could cause Roosevelt and the party great embarrassment and harm. "I want white supremacy . . . but I want to put it before the people in the way Colonel Roosevelt put it before the people," Hale explained. Describing Roosevelt's letter on the Negro question, he said that when plucked of its embellishments, it simply said: "Get out of here, we don't want you." But with the camouflaging verbiage, Hale praised the letter as a masterpiece of rhetorical shrewdness. Thus, he explained, the whole Negro question was just a matter of being tactful and considering what was good for Roosevelt's candidacy. That meant, he continued, trying to convince both North and South that Progressives were sincere in solving the Negro problem—solving it, of course, according to the accepted methods of the respective sections.[36] In effect, the only difference between southern and northern Progressives was that one wanted to assault the Negro in broad daylight and strip him of all his rights; the other wanted, like a gentle thief under cover of darkness, to relieve him quietly of his extraneous civic and social baggage.

When the Progressive convention opened in Chicago, anxious NAACP officials were there carrying a Negro-rights plank to be fitted into the Progressive platform.[37] Without much ado, the platform committee discarded the plank. Only committeewoman Jane Addams stridently objected to making the Progressive party "lily-white," but even she calmed down enough to make a seconding speech for Roosevelt in which she praised the "splendid platform" and unblemished leader of the "Bull Moose" party.[38]

After Roosevelt's cavalier treatment of the southern Negro, he attempted in his Chicago acceptance speech to appease the northern Negro. Clearly his objective was to harvest the Negro vote in the North and the white vote in the South.[39] At any rate, few Negroes or Negrophiles were fooled by Roosevelt's cunning. The *Independent* was indignant. "A bull is an unwelcome apparition in a china shop," the *Independent* wrote, "and the Progressive party convention gave no kindlier welcome to the Negro question."[40] Not until 1916 was the Progressive party to include in its platform a plank calling for the equal treatment of all people regardless of "race, creed, or nativity"; but by that time the party would have suffered the calamity of oblivion.[41]

Rebuffed by the Progressive and Republican parties, many Negroes turned in desperation to Woodrow Wilson, the Democratic nominee. Villard, who strongly supported Wilson's candidacy, urged him to make a statement favorable to the Negro. After great soul-searching, Wilson obliged. In a letter on October 16 to Bishop Alexander Walters, a Negro spokesman, he wrote that if elected he would seek for the Negro "not mere grudging justice, but justice with liberality and cordial good feelings." Before a committee of Negroes Wilson pledged that he would "seek to be President of the whole nation and would know no differences of race or creed or section, but to act in good conscience and in Christian spirit through it all."[42]

Expecting a close race, the Democratic party went to unprecedented lengths to get the Negro vote. The Democratic campaign headquarters of New York expended $52,255 in courting black ballots. Ironically, as events soon proved, for the first time in their history many Negroes abandoned the tradition that the Republican party was the ship and all else the sea and voted for Wilson. Even the wary DuBois, who doubted that Wilson loved Negroes, voted Democratic. Though there was no precise way

77

of knowing, estimates gave Wilson 100,000 colored votes. The two-faced strategy of the Progressive party failed as the Negro voted either for Taft or Wilson. Therefore, Roosevelt did worse in the South than he had in 1904.[43]

With the Republican party split, 1912 was a year of victory for the Democratic party. And in the excitement of victory, Wilson seemingly forgot the assurances he had given the Negro in the throes of the campaign. Villard, who had campaigned strenuously for Wilson, sought the new president's approval for a national race commission as a reward for his service. The commission was to make an exhaustive and scientific study of race relations in the United States and suggest devices for bettering the perilous situation. On May 4, Villard left an outline of his plan with Wilson. Then throughout the long summer, the persistent editor tried to arrange an interview with the president to discuss his plans; but he found the White House door closed to him. On August 19 Wilson sent Villard a letter indicating that the race commission which he envisioned would be a great social blunder because the South would interpret it as an indictment. Furthermore, Wilson complained that he had so many things on his mind that an interview with him would be unprofitable at that time. Two days later Wilson wrote Villard another letter flatly turning down his request for a race commission. He maintained that he was "absolutely blocked by the sentiment of Senators; not alone Senators from the South by any means, but Senators from various parts of the country."[44]

Not until October 7 did Villard receive an appointment to see the president. In his memoirs Villard recorded that it was a long but fruitless talk, for the two were poles apart in their racial attitudes. As an excuse for inactivity, Wilson pleaded humble inability to handle the race problem. "I say it with shame and humiliation," Wilson lamented; "but I have thought about this thing for twenty years and I see no way out. It will take a very big man to solve this thing."[45] In years to come, Wilson would feel that he had sufficient stature to make the whole world "safe for democracy"; but he paled before the problem of making America safe for the Negro. ⟩ *Satire*

Meanwhile, throughout the summer of 1913, Wilson lost no time in dousing the fires of Negro hopes that he had built up with flowery, if insubstantial, promises. Within a short time after taking office, Wilson set a new precedent by segregating the Post Office and the Department of the Treasury, for years fortresses of Negro employment with dignity. Washington, the black Mecca above the Potomac, reverted from a free city to a metropolis of two distinct classes of people based on the ultimate criterion of color.

The Democratic administration of Wilson brought a spectacular change in the atmosphere of the capital city. Arriving with the presidential baggage was a procession of southern attendants such as William G. MacAdoo of Georgia, Josephus Daniels of North Carolina, and Colonel Edward M. House of Texas—all of whom spoke the unmistakable race idioms of the South. Ambassadorships went to Thomas Nelson Page of Virginia and Walter Hines Page of North Carolina. Still presiding over the Supreme Court was Chief Justice Edward D. White of Louisiana. In Congress an Alabamian was Senate majority leader, and in the House a Virginian performed the leadership role. The change was as though southern generals had suddenly usurped the leadership of the Union Army.

Many northern supporters of Wilson, particularly political independents, attributed Wilson's segregationist policy to his southern subordinates.[46] For instance, Secretary of the Treasury MacAdoo staunchly defended the innovation of segregation in his department. "I shall not be a party," he declared, "to the enforced and unwelcome juxtaposition of white and colored employees."[47] Southern segregationists did not, however, coerce Wilson down unwanted paths; for he was in full stride with them. The president had an extravagant love for the South which seemed to increase in direct proportion to his distance and time away from it.[48]

As president of Princeton, Wilson had drawn the color line; and as governor of New Jersey, he had denied any recognition to the Negro. Once in the executive mansion, he was amenable to advice from such persons as his old friend Thomas ("Clansman") Dixon. On July 29, 1913, Dixon wrote to Wilson complaining about a Negro appointee who was in a position "to boss white girls." Wilson replied that he was doing everything in his power to see that there was a complete separation of the races.[49] Nor was color the only basis of discrimination for Wilson, for he also approved of discrimination based on sex. Perhaps on account of his southern heritage, he frowned upon woman suffrage; but he slyly evaded the issue by declaring that it was a matter for the states to decide.[50]

As pointed out already by Booker Washington's observation, the discriminatory policies of the president aroused great bitterness among Negro leaders. When in 1914 William Monroe Trotter, a Negro journalist and spokesman, visited the White House to complain about segregation in federal departments, Wilson harried him out of his presence with charges of insolence and improprieties. Quite clearly, racial and religious prejudice gained wider currency as southerners attained ascendancy in the national government. After many Negroes had jumped party traces for the first time to vote for Wilson, he flung them overboard apparently without a moral qualm. As the *New Republic* neatly and concisely phrased it: "The President used fair words in 1912 in his appeal to the Negroes for votes. We know now that those words meant nothing."[51]

As an anticlimax to an era of Negro disillusionment, the Wilson Congress of 1913-1915 handled a torrent of bills proposing discriminatory legislation against Negroes, more than any other Congress in American history. At least twenty bills called for segregation of all public carriers in Washington, D.C.

Other bills called for the banning of Negroes from the Army and Navy and for the prohibition of Negro and white intermarriages, although these bills failed to pass.[52] An era that had started out seemingly so opportune for the Negro had ended in utter dejection. For men of color, the Square Deal and the New Freedom contained little that was square and little that was freedom. In retrospect, the Booker Washington dinner, the Crum appointment, and Wilson's pro-Negro statements of 1912—all celebrated as great Negro triumphs—had merely been aberrations, certainly not the normal events of the Progressive era.

VI

CONCLUSION

Historians of the progressive movement have given only passing notice of its relationship to racism. Yet racism flourished during the enthusiastic years of progressive reform. Although historians have acknowledged that the messengers of southern progressivism spoke in the tongues of racist demagogues, there has been almost no recognition of the racial attitudes of northern progressives. But as racism reached its southern climax in the early years of the twentieth century, it spilled unchallenged over the Mason-Dixon line. Many terrorized and discouraged Negroes who sought refuge in the crusading North found no respite from brazen violence and the ubiquitous shibboleths of white suprem-

82

acy. Nor did the rise of progressivism alleviate the deteriorating status of the Negro. On the contrary, progressivism actually hastened the triumph of racism.

By the turn of the century the North had long since wearied of the vexing Negro question. The common attitude was that the North had given the Negro freedom, and now the Negro had to prove his worthiness for it. Anyway, the North was much more interested in the pursuit of the tantalizing dollar. Southerners, however, dwelt implacably on the Negro problem, angling here and there until they landed what they considered the final solution. Whereas slavery had once provided the ultimate in social perfection, the second "peculiar institution" of the South relied on legal disfranchisement, rigid segregation, and occasional violence to keep the colored man "in his place." As one writer summed it up: "The Northern Hare ran swiftly, when it did run, along the course of Southern Reconstruction, but it did not endure to the end. Whereas the Southern Tortoise, slow but sure, has kept its equal pace. . . . It did not weary of the everlasting Negro Question."[1] As in the fable, the indefatigable southern turtle prevailed; and even more, it converted the rabbit to its reptilian habits.

Although northern progressives raised the specter of humanitarianism, their altruism—with the exception of that of the new abolitionists—fell miserably short of the color line. If there were no justifiable excuses for their inactivity on the part of the Negro, there were many reasons. The progressive generation grew up in an era that widely dramatized the licentiousness and barbarities of the Negro. Historians stereotyped Reconstruction as the dark age of American history. In 1913 James Ford Rhodes stated that "no large policy" in the country had been so blatant a debacle as Black Reconstruction.[2] The immigration problem, the Achilles heel of northern liberals, caused many a progressive to adopt racist theories. Though combating Darwinian sociology on one hand, progressives declared the struggle of the lower species analogous to the "struggle of the races." In addition, many progressive stalwarts such as Albert J. Beveridge of Indiana held that the doctrine of Anglo-Saxon superiority was more dear than human rights. The Declaration of Independence, he claimed, was not applicable to non-Anglo-Saxons, because it was written "by self-governing men for self-governing men."[3] As Lincoln's biographer, Beveridge no doubt would have liked to have reworded the Gettysburg Address to read "government of Anglo-Saxons, by Anglo-Saxons, for Anglo-Saxons."

On the national scene, Roosevelt and Wilson hardly embodied the progressive mystique, though both were adept at taking on the coloring of their surroundings. When they were in a position where they might have ameliorated the racial situation and assisted the hapless Negro, they instead smoothed the path for a racist stampede. After 1904, at the expense of the Negro, Roosevelt groveled to reconciliate the white South. Once a falling out of white men had given the Negro freedom, and now a binding up of sectional wounds brought catastrophic results to the black man. Moreover, in 1912 the coming of Wilson's administration represented a major revolution in the geographical distribution of political power. Southerners, for the first time since the 1850's, occupied the commanding positions of national authority. The decline of the Negro followed accordingly.

Racism was not by any means confined to America, but was a part of a larger and therefore more reprehensible picture. England's Rudyard Kipling gloriously versified the unctuous credo of the "white man's burden." On the continent, Friedrich Nietzsche and Houston Chamberlain were laying the ideological groundwork for Nazism and its sinister corollary, anti-Semitism. Madison Grant, a noted American biologist and author, called for all Caucasians to stand at Armageddon and battle for world supremacy. The white race, he warned, must "shake off the shackles of inveterate altruism, discard the vain phantom of internationalism, and reassert pride of race and the right of merit to rule."[4] Truly it was a world obsessed with race.

In sum, the supreme blind spot of the progressives, North and South alike, was the Negro problem. And although racism reached its sordid climax in the twenties, a fertile seedbed had been prepared in the heralded period of enlightened reform known as the Progressive era. In 1915 on Thanksgiving night, the burning of a cross atop Stone Mountain in Georgia had marked the resurrection of the Ku Klux Klan, an event symbolic of the preceding, as well as a future, era. The rebirth of the Invisible Empire was also an event which characterized far too much of American history. And only in such a context can one understand today the urgent and unrelenting (if sometimes irresponsible) quest of the Negro for justice.

NOTES

INTRODUCTION

1 For example, see George Mowry, *Theodore Roosevelt and the Progressive Movement* (Madison: The University of Wisconsin Press, 1947); Russel B. Nye, *Midwestern Progressive Politics* (Lansing: Michigan State University Press, 1959); Harold Underwood Faulkner, *The Quest for Social Justice, 1898-1914* (New York: Macmillan Co., 1937).

CHAPTER I

1 Quoted in Eric Goldman, *Rendezvous with Destiny: A History of Modern American Reform* (1st ed. New York: Alfred A. Knopf, 1952), p. 177.
2 *Ibid.*
3 C. Vann Woodward's *The Strange Career of Jim Crow* (New York: Oxford University Press, 1957) best traces the rise of racism in the South; for a divergent view see Kenneth M. Stampp, *The Era of Reconstruction, 1865-*

1877 (New York: Alfred A. Knopf, 1965), p. 82. Stampp states that ". . . before the radical program began [1867], the Johnson governments themselves had introduced the whole pattern of disenfranchisement, discrimination, and segregation into the postwar South."

4 Samuel Denny Smith, *The Negro in Congress, 1870-1901* (Chapel Hill: The University of North Carolina Press, 1940), p. 39.

5 Hampton M. Jarrell, *Wade Hampton and the Negro* (Columbia: University of South Carolina Press, 1950), pp. 73, 122.

6 *Ibid.*, p. 123.

7 *Ibid.*, p. 135.

8 C. Vann Woodward, *Reunion and Reaction* (1st ed. Boston: Little, Brown and Co., 1951), p. 25.

9 Thomas Wentworth Higginson, August 13, 1861, to his mother, *Letters and Journals of Thomas Wentworth Higginson, 1846-1906*, edited by Mary Thacher Higginson (Boston: Houghton Mifflin Co., 1921), pp. 156, 158-59.

10 Woodward, *Strange Career of Jim Crow*, p. 17.

11 *Ibid.*, p. 34.

12 Quoted in Nathaniel Weyl, *The Negro in American Civilization* (Washington: Public Affairs Press, 1960), p. 108.

13 George Brown Tindall, *South Carolina Negroes, 1877-1900* (Columbia: University of South Carolina Press, 1952), p. 293.

14 C. Vann Woodward, "Tom Watson and the Negro in Agrarian Politics," *Journal of Southern History*, IV (February 1938), 18-19.

15 Paul Lewinson, *Race, Class, and Party* (New York: Oxford University Press, 1932), p. 77.

16 *Ibid.*, p. 79.

17 Mississippi was the only state to disfranchise the Negro before the frustration of the agrarian crusade.

18 Disfranchisement dates: South Carolina, 1895; Louisiana, 1897; North Carolina, 1900 and 1905; Alabama and Virginia, 1901; Georgia, 1908; Oklahoma, 1910.

19 The United States Supreme Court ruled the "grandfather clause" unconstitutional in 1915.

20 Quoted in Lewinson, *Race, Class, and Party*, p. 84.

21 *Ibid.*

22 *Ibid.*, p. 86.

23 *Ibid.*, p. 81.

24 Ray Stannard Baker, *Following the Color Line* (New York: Doubleday, Page and Co., 1908), p. 236.

25 *Ibid.*, p. 237.

26 Quoted in Tindall, *South Carolina Negroes*, pp. 251-52.

27 *Ibid.*, p. 255.

28 *Ibid.*, p. 258.

29 C. Vann Woodward, *Origins of the New South, 1877-1913*, Vol. IX of *A History of the South*, edited by Wendell Holmes Stephenson and E. Merton Coulter (Baton Rouge: Louisiana State University Press, 1951), p. 350; Jerome McDuffie, "The Wilmington Riots of November 10, 1898" (unpub-

lished master's thesis, Wake Forest College, 1963), p. 150. McDuffie's view is, however, that Wilmington's riot was not racial but political.

30 Baker, *Following the Color Line*, p. 245; Dewey W. Grantham, Jr., "Hoke Smith, Progressive Governor of Georgia, 1907-1909," *Journal of Southern History*, XV (November 1949), 426; Woodward, "Tom Watson and the Negro," 32.

31 Thomas F. Gossett, *Race: The History of an Idea in America* (Dallas: Southern Methodist University Press, 1963), pp. 269-70; Southern Race Commission on the Study of Lynching, *Lynchings and What They Mean* (Atlanta: The Commission, 1931), p. 73.

32 James Elbert Cutler, "The Practice of Lynching in the United States," *South Atlantic Quarterly*, VI (April 1907), 134.

33 Woodward, *Strange Career of Jim Crow*, p. 49.

34 *Ibid.*, pp. 81-87.

35 Clarence Poe, "What Is Justice between White Man and Black Man in the Rural South?" in *Lectures and Addresses on the Negro in the South* (Charlottesville: The Michie Co., n.d.), pp. 45-47.

36 Tindall, *South Carolina Negroes*, p. 216.

37 Unsigned review, "Race Problems Knocking at the Doors of Congress," *Current Opinion*, LIV (February 1913), 96.

38 Samuel R. Spencer, Jr., *Booker T. Washington and the Negro's Place in American Life* (Boston: Little, Brown and Co., 1955), p. 98.

39 Quoted in Rayford W. Logan, *The Negro in American Life and Thought* (New York: The Dial Press, 1954), p. 279.

40 Spencer, *Booker T. Washington*, p. 105.

41 Quoted in Goldman, *Rendezvous with Destiny*, p. 177.

42 Woodward, *Strange Career of Jim Crow*, p. 56, claims that had northern opinion been running contrary to southern racism, it would have "broken feebly instead of becoming a wave of the future."

43 New York *Tribune*, April 7, 1877.

44 See, for example, Robert Franklin Durden, *James Shepherd Pike: Republicanism and the American Negro, 1850-1882* (Durham: Duke University Press, 1957), p. ix and *passim*.

45 William Alexander Mabry, "Disfranchisement of the Negro in Mississippi," *Journal of Southern History*, IV (August 1938), 322; John A. Garraty, *Henry Cabot Lodge* (New York: Alfred A. Knopf, 1953), pp. 119-20. In a recent article, Richard E. Welch, Jr., "The Federal Election Bill of 1890: Postscripts and Prelude," *The Journal of American History*, LII (December 1965), 511, points out the contradiction in the standard liberal interpretation of history which applauds recent federal efforts to ensure greater political equality for the Negro while deploring the Election Bill of 1890 as a "Force Bill."

46 Frank W. Quillan, *The Color Line in Ohio* (Ann Arbor: George Wahr, 1913), pp. 149-51, 160.

47 Quoted in Baker, *Following the Color Line*, p. 130.

48 Charles H. Wesley, *Negro Labor in the United States, 1850-1925* (New York: Vanguard Press, 1927), p. 231.

49 Quillan, *Color Line in Ohio*, p. 144.
50 Baker, *Following the Color Line*, p. 267.
51 Raymond A. Cook, "The Man Behind 'The Birth of a Nation,' " *North Carolina Historical Review*, XXXIX (Autumn 1962), 524, 533-34, 540.
52 George F. Hoar, *Autobiography of Seventy Years* (New York: Charles Scribner's Sons, 1903), II, 150-51.
53 Thomas Pearce Bailey, *Race Orthodoxy in the South* (New York: The Neale Publishing Co., 1914), p. 29.
54 Unsigned review, "Is the Race Problem Insoluble?" *Independent*, LX (June 21, 1906), 1495-96.

CHAPTER II

1 Seth M. Scheiner, "Theodore Roosevelt and the Negro, 1901-1908," *Journal of Negro History*, XLVII (July 1962), 176.
2 John Hope Franklin, *From Slavery to Freedom* (New York: Alfred A. Knopf, 1948), p. 428.
3 W. E. B. DuBois, *The Souls of Black Folk* (3rd ed. Chicago: A. C. McClurg & Co., 1903), p. 175.
4 Woodrow Wilson, *The New Freedom*, edited by William E. Leuchtenburg (Englewood Cliffs: Prentice-Hall, Inc., 1961), p. 168.
5 Walter Rauschenbusch, *Christianizing the Social Order* (New York: Macmillan Co., 1912), p. 2.
6 Robert H. Wiebe, *Businessmen and Reform: A Study of the Progressive Movement* (Cambridge: Harvard University Press, 1962), p. 107. Typical of the relation of some senators to business interests, Senator Stephen B. Elkins of West Virginia in 1907 asked James Stillman, a Wall Street financier, for a liberal extension of his loan in a letter itemizing a long list of services he had performed for the shrine of private finance.
7 New York *Times*, September 15, 1901.
8 William Allen White, *The Old Order Changeth* (New York: Macmillan Co., 1912), pp. 29-30.
9 Wiebe, *Businessmen and Reform*, p. 179.
10 For example, see Gabriel Kolko, *The Triumph of Conservatism: A Reinterpretation of American History, 1900-1916* (London: The Free Press of Glencoe, 1963), p. 61 and *passim*. Kolko's key statement is "The pervasive reality of the period [1900-1916] is big business' control of politics set in the context of the political regulation of the economy." Kolko's argument that there was no Progressive era is largely a matter of academic hairsplitting. He concludes that because business supported limited reform and because Roosevelt and Wilson had conservative tendencies, the whole period was conservative. Kolko discounts that "half-loaf" measures can be progressive and that an era is judged not only by legislation passed but also by the thinking of its articulate people. In this sense, *progressive* was no misnomer for the period.
11 *Ibid.*, p. 111.

12 *Ibid.,* p. 209; Wilson, *The New Freedom,* p. 8.

13 Kolko, *Triumph of Conservatism,* p. 216.

14 Amos Pinchot, *The History of the Progressive Party, 1912-1916,* edited by H. M. Hooker (New York: New York University Press, 1958), p. 165.

15 White, *Old Order Changeth,* p. 53.

16 Wiebe, *Businessmen and Reform,* pp. 6-7.

17 Quoted in Nye, *Midwestern Progressive Politics,* p. 187.

18 C. C. Regier, *The Era of the Muckrakers* (Chapel Hill: The University of North Carolina Press, 1932), pp. 55-56.

19 Frederic C. Howe, *The Confessions of a Reformer* (New York: Charles Scribner's Sons, 1925), *passim;* also see Brand Whitlock, *Forty Years of It* (New York: D. Appleton and Co., 1914), for an example of a reform mayor in Toledo, Ohio. Whitlock served as mayor of Toledo from 1905 to 1911, taking over the position from another reform mayor of some note named "Golden Rule" Jones.

20 Robert S. Maxwell, *La Follette and the Rise of the Progressives in Wisconsin* (Madison: State Historical Society of Wisconsin, 1956), p. 28.

21 *Ibid.,* pp. 74-76, 85-86, 129-30.

22 Kolko, *Triumph of Conservatism,* pp. 212-13.

23 Howe, *Confessions of a Reformer,* pp. 196-97.

24 La Follette's *Autobiography* (Madison: Robert M. La Follette Co., 1913) is probably the best statement of his views, or lack of them, on the matters.

25 Mowry, *Theodore Roosevelt,* p. 18.

26 Quoted in Richard Hofstadter, *The Age of Reform: From Bryan to F. D. R.* (1st ed. New York: Alfred A. Knopf, 1955), p. 233.

27 Charles Forcey, *The Crossroads of Liberalism* (New York: Oxford University Press, 1961), pp. 6, 11, 18-20.

28 Herbert Croly, *The Promise of American Life* (New York: Macmillan Co., 1909), pp. 20-21, 152-53; Forcey, *Crossroads,* p. 29.

29 Forcey, *Crossroads,* pp. 36, 46.

30 *Ibid.,* p. 36.

31 Goldman, *Rendezvous with Destiny,* p. 203. For an overview of the relevance of Croly to New Deal and present political theory, see Byron Dexter, "Herbert Croly and the Promise of American Life," *Political Science Quarterly,* LXX (June 1955), 197-218.

32 Hofstadter, *Age of Reform,* p. 176.

33 William E. Leuchtenburg, "Progressivism and Imperialism: The Progressive Movement and Foreign Policy, 1898-1916," *Mississippi Valley Historical Review,* XXXIX (December 1952), 483-504.

34 Forcey, *Crossroads,* p. xxiii.

35 Mowry, *Theodore Roosevelt,* pp. 42, 92-93.

36 *Ibid.,* pp. 143-44.

37 Faulkner, *The Quest for Social Justice,* p. 108.

38 Herbert Croly, *Progressive Democracy* (New York: Macmillan Co., 1914), p. 409.

39 Walter Weyl, *The New Democracy* (New York: Macmillan Co., 1912), pp. 319, 321, 338-39. Roosevelt cited Croly's *The Promise of American Life* and Weyl's *The New Democracy* as the true books of progressivism.
40 Ralph H. Gabriel, *The Course of American Democratic Thought* (New York: The Ronald Press Co., 1940), pp. 328-32.
41 Rauschenbusch, *Christianizing the Social Order*, p. 96.
42 *Ibid.*, p. 5.
43 White, *Old Order Changeth*, p. 144.
44 "Official Minutes of the First National Convention of the Progressive Party," p. 3, Theodore Roosevelt MSS, Library of Congress.
45 *Ibid.*, p. 13.
46 Pinchot, *Progressive Party*, p. 171.
47 Allen F. Davis, "The Social Workers and the Progressive Party, 1912-1916," *American Historical Review*, LXIX (April 1964), 673, 678.
48 Wilson, *The New Freedom*, pp. 27-28, 164.
49 *Ibid.*, pp. 51, 131, 159.

CHAPTER III

1 Fred H. Matthews, "White Community and 'Yellow Peril,'" *Mississippi Valley Historical Review*, L (March 1964), 619.
2 Treated in Chapter IV.
3 Ira V. Brown, "Lyman Abbott and Freedmen's Aid," *Journal of Southern History*, XV (February 1949), 30.
4 *Ibid.*, 30, 33.
5 William Warren Sweet, *Makers of Christianity* (New York: H. Holt and Co., 1937), III, 320.
6 Lyman Abbott, *Reminiscences* (Boston: Houghton Mifflin Co., 1915), p. ix.
7 *Ibid.*, pp. 420-21, 431, 437-38.
8 *Ibid.*, p. 235.
9 Lyman Abbott, *America in the Making* (New Haven: Yale University Press, 1911), pp. 173-74.
10 *Ibid.*, p. 217.
11 *Ibid.*
12 Abbott, *Reminiscences*, p. 424.
13 Carl Schurz, *The Autobiography of Carl Schurz*, abridgement by Wayne Andrews (New York: Charles Scribner's Sons, 1961), p. 188; Carl Schurz, *Speeches, Correspondence and Political Papers*, edited by Frederic Bancroft (New York: G. P. Putnam's Sons, 1913), I, 197 (hereafter referred to as *Speeches*).
14 Schurz, *Speeches*, I, 197.
15 Schurz, *Autobiography*, p. 188.
16 Schurz, *Speeches*, I, 269; Carl Schurz to his wife, 27 August, 1865, Jackson, Mississippi, *ibid.*
17 *Ibid.*, I, 367.

18 Carl Schurz to his wife, 27 August, 1865, Jackson, Mississippi, *ibid.*, I, 269.
19 Claude Moore Fuess, *Carl Schurz, Reformer* (Port Washington: Kennikat Press, Inc., 1963), p. 379.
20 Carl Schurz to Theodore Roosevelt, 29 December, 1903, New York, *Speeches*, VI, 310.
21 Carl Schurz, "Can the South Solve the Negro Problem?" *McClure's Magazine*, XXII (January 1904), 275.
22 Charles Francis Adams, Jr., *Lee at Appomattox and Other Papers* (2nd ed. enlarged. Boston: Houghton Mifflin Co., 1902), pp. 427-29.
23 Charles Francis Adams, Jr., *An Autobiography* (Boston: Houghton Mifflin Co., 1916), pp. 190-95.
24 Charles Francis Adams, Jr., "Reflex Light from Africa," *The Century Magazine*, LXXII (1906), 102, 105.
25 *Ibid.*, 107.
26 Adams, *Autobiography*, p. 217.
27 Baker, *Following the Color Line*, p. 301.
28 Ray Stannard Baker, "The Color Line in the North," *American Magazine*, LXV (1908), 349.
29 Baker, *Following the Color Line*, p. 268.
30 *Ibid.*, p. 8.
31 *Ibid.*, facing p. 7.
32 *Ibid.*, p. 306.
33 Ray Stannard Baker, "Negro Suffrage in a Democracy," *Atlantic Monthly*, CVI (November 1910), 615-16; Baker, *Following the Color Line*, p. 240.
34 Baker, *Following the Color Line*, p. 242.
35 Ray Stannard Baker, "What Is Lynching?" *McClure's Magazine*, XXIV (January 1905), 314.
36 Baker, *Following the Color Line*, p. 293.
37 *Ibid.*, pp. 290, 305.
38 Thomas Nelson Page, "The Negro: The Southerners' Problem," *McClure's Magazine*, XXII (April 1904), 619-26; Gossett, *Race*, p. 273.
39 William B. Conant, "The Future of the Negro," *The Arena*, XL (July 1908), 65.
40 Andrew Sledd, "The Negro: Another View," *Atlantic Monthly*, XC (July 1902), 73.
41 Walter L. Hawley, "Passing of the Race Problem," *The Arena*, XXIV (November 1900), 469, 478.
42 Unsigned review, "The Real Interest of the Negro," *The American Review of Reviews*, XXVII (February 1903), 149.
43 William Hemstreet, "The Problem of the Blacks," *The Arena*, XXIX (May 1903), 499.
44 Walter Winston Kenilworth, "Negro Influence in American Life," *Forum*, XLVI (1911), 177-78.
45 *Ibid.*, 171.
46 James Boyle, "Has the Fifteenth Amendment Been Justified?" *The Arena*, XXXI (May 1904), 482.
47 Editorial, *The American Review of Reviews*, XXVIII (August 1903), 138.

48 Unsigned review, "Changed Opinions on the Race Question," *The World's Work*, V (1903), 3156.
49 Editorial, *Outlook*, LXXIII (April 25, 1903), 951.
50 Edward Atkinson, "The Negro as a Beast," *North American Review*, CLXXXI (August 1905), 203-4, 215.
51 Baker, *Following the Color Line*, p. 263.
52 Unsigned review, "Lynching and Public Sentiment," *Outlook*, XCVIII (June 10, 1911), 290.
53 Robert Bennett Bean, M.D., "The Negro Brain," *The Century Magazine*, LXXII (1906), 784. Dr. Bean's theory is reminiscent of Josiah Clark Nott, a southern physician who in 1854 published *Types of Mankind*. This volume of 800 pages went quickly through ten editions at the exorbitant price of $7.50. Nott theorized that there were separate species of men, such as the Negro, who were incapable of civilization. See Gossett, *Race*, p. 65.
54 The noblest opponent of racist science was Dr. Franz Boas, a brilliant anthropologist, who in *The Mind of Primitive Man* (New York: Macmillan Co., 1911) set the pace for all subsequent serious work in his field. Boaz firmly asserted that intelligence could not be established along racial lines. Often his book is called the Magna Carta of racial equality.
55 Unsigned review, "Fifty Years of Freedom," *The World's Work*, XXVI (June 1913), 149.
56 Unsigned review, "Race Problems Knocking at the Doors of Congress," 96.
57 Gossett, *Race*, p. 114.
58 Albert Bushnell Hart, head of the Harvard Department of History and a prolific writer on American politics, was another influential professor who taught racism. About the Negro, he surmised: "If as many people supposed, the negro were a black white man, a belated scion of civilization, the race problem would now be very different." See Albert B. Hart, "The Outcome of the Southern Race Question," *North American Review*, CLXXXVIII (July 1908), 51.
59 Howe, *Confessions of a Reformer*, p. 7.
60 Gossett, *Race*, p. 146; see also Richard Hofstadter, *Social Darwinism in American Thought, 1860-1915* (Philadelphia: University of Pennsylvania Press, 1944), *passim.*
61 Quoted in Nye, *Midwestern Progressive Politics*, p. 29.
62 William Graham Sumner, *Folkways* (Boston: Ginn & Co., 1907), p. 78.
63 Gossett, *Race*, p. 154.
64 *Ibid.*, p. 169.
65 Edward A. Ross, *The Old World in the New* (New York: The Century Co., 1914), pp. 219-27, 272-87.
66 Edward A. Ross, "The Causes of Race Superiority," *Annals of the American Academy of Political and Social Science*, XVIII (July 1901), 85.
67 Maxwell, *La Follette*, pp. 58, 81, 139, 144, 159.
68 Henry Steele Commager, *The American Mind: An Interpretation of American Thought and Character since 1880* (New Haven: Yale University Press, 1950), p. 246.

69 John R. Commons, *Races and Immigrants* (New York: Macmillan Co., 1907), pp. 46-48, 136.
70 Josiah Royce, *Race Questions, Provincialism, and Other American Problems* (New York: Macmillan Co., 1908), pp. 9-14, 33-36, 45, 53.
71 *Ibid.*, pp. 15, 18-19.
72 Croly, *Promise of American Life*, p. 81.
73 Forcey, *Crossroads*, p. 97; Walter Lippmann, *A Preface to Politics* (New York: Mitchell Kennerley, 1914), *passim*, especially pp. 202, 236.
74 Weyl, *New Democracy*, pp. 180, 342.
75 *Ibid.*, pp. 343-45.
76 *Ibid.*, pp. 344-46.

CHAPTER IV

1 Quoted in Spencer, *Booker T. Washington*, p. 144.
2 DuBois, *Black Folk*, pp. vii, 2-3.
3 Quoted in Goldman, *Rendezvous with Destiny*, p. 179; Spencer, *Booker T. Washington*, pp. 155-56.
4 DuBois, *Black Folk*, p. 51.
5 Quoted in Weyl, *Negro in American Civilization*, p. 120.
6 Unsigned review, "The Platform of the Outlook," *Outlook*, LXXXIV (September 1, 1906), 4. "On the whole," the *Outlook* wrote, "we think the Niagara Movement would be more useful if it demanded more of the Negro race and put less emphasis on its demands for the Negro race."
7 Robert Livingston Schuyler, editor, *Dictionary of American Biography* (New York: Charles Scribner's Sons, 1958), XXII, Supp. Two, 689. Walling was a wealthy Kentuckian whose father was the Democratic vice-presidential nominee in 1880. He had a degree from the University of Chicago and studied at the Harvard Law School. He was a true humanitarian intensely interested in the Negro problem. He died in Europe in 1936 while helping to evacuate refugees from Nazi terror.
8 William E. Walling, "The Race War in the North," *Independent*, LXV (September 3, 1908), 529, 531.
9 Mary White Ovington, *The Walls Came Tumbling Down* (New York: Harcourt, Brace and Co., 1947), p. 102.
10 Walling, "Race War," 530-32.
11 *Ibid.*, 534.
12 Probably ample proof of Villard's honest and independent reporting is attested by Roosevelt's criticism of him: "From Villard down I regard the editors of that paper [*Evening Post*] as very much worse than spoils politicians. . . ." Roosevelt further described Villard as "dishonest" and a thoroughly "bad citizen." See Theodore Roosevelt, *The Letters of Theodore Roosevelt*, edited by Elting Morison (Cambridge: Harvard University Press, 1951), II, 1184.
13 Oswald Garrison Villard, *Fighting Years: Memoirs of a Liberal Editor* (New York: Harcourt, Brace and Co., 1939), p. 173.

14 Ovington, *The Walls*, p. 103.
15 Villard, *Fighting Years*, p. 193.
16 New York *Times*, February 13, 1909.
17 *Ibid.*
18 *Ibid.*
19 Franklin, *Slavery to Freedom*, p. 439.
20 M. A. DeWolfe Howe, *Portrait of an Independent: Moorfield Storey, 1845-1929* (Boston: Houghton Mifflin Co., 1932), p. 191 and *passim*.
21 *Ibid.*, pp. 191-98. Storey held that there was a crass, un-Christian materialism behind American imperialism. In 1898 he wrote: "We reached out for Cuba and if the Teller Resolution had not been passed by the Senate at the end of the war, we would have seized Cuba."
22 *Ibid.*, pp. 193, 234, 264.
23 *Ibid.*, pp. 255-57.
24 Jane Addams, "Has the Emancipation Act Been Nullified by National Indifference?" *The Survey*, XXIX (February 1, 1913), 565-66.
25 Dumas Malone, editor, *Dictionary of American Biography* (New York: Charles Scribner's Sons, 1936), XIX, 442-43. Ward was a superbly precocious child. He could read the Bible in Hebrew between the ages of six and nine; he accomplished the same feat in Greek and Latin by fifteen. Later he learned a number of Semitic languages in connection with his studies of ancient civilization.
26 Unsigned review, "The Worst Opprest," *Independent*, LXXIII (August 22, 1912), 448.
27 Unsigned review, "Secretary Taft as Conciliator," *Independent*, LXIV (March 19, 1908), 696-97.
28 *Ibid.*
29 Kelly Miller, *Race Adjustment: Essays on the Negro in America* (New York: The Neale Publishing Co., 1908), p. 40.
30 DuBois, *Black Folk*, p. 106.
31 Quoted in Goldman, *Rendezvous with Destiny*, p. 99.
32 In 1925 Darrow, opposing William Jennings Bryan, provided the defense in the heralded Scopes trial in which he defended a teacher charged with teaching evolution. See Frederick Lewis Allen, *Only Yesterday* (New York: Harper and Row, 1931), pp. 201-3.
33 Quoted in Goldman, *Rendezvous with Destiny*, p. 125.
34 Quoted in Irving Stone, *Clarence Darrow for the Defense* (New York: Doubleday Co., 1941), p. 170.
35 Quoted in Goldman, *Rendezvous with Destiny*, p. 128.
36 William E. Walling, "Science and Human Brotherhood," *Independent*, LXVI (1909), 1324, 1326.
37 William Allen White to John S. Phillips, 20 August, 1912, *Selected Letters of William White, 1899-1943*, edited by Walter Johnson (New York: H. Holt and Co., 1947), p. 136.
38 New York *Times*, March 31, 1911.

CHAPTER V

1 For example, George Mowry, *The Era of Theodore Roosevelt, 1900-1912* (New York: Harper and Brothers, 1958), p. 165, writes: "Of Roosevelt's sincerity in this matter [Negro rights] there can be little doubt."

2 Quoted in Owen Wister, *Roosevelt, the Story of a Friendship* (New York: Macmillan Co., 1930), p. 253.

3 Quoted in Arthur S. Link, *Woodrow Wilson and the Progressive Era* (New York: Harper and Brothers, 1954), p. 65; Villard, *Fighting Years*, p. 237.

4 Franklin, *Slavery to Freedom*, p. 428.

5 *Ibid.*

6 Mowry, *Era of Theodore Roosevelt*, p. 166.

7 Henry F. Pringle, *Theodore Roosevelt: A Biography* (New York: Harcourt, Brace and Co., 1931), p. 344.

8 Spencer, *Booker T. Washington*, pp. 137-38.

9 Thomas Nelson Page, "President Roosevelt from the Standpoint of a Southern Democrat," *Metropolitan Magazine*, XXI (1905), 680.

10 William Garrott Brown, "President Roosevelt and the South," *Independent*, LIX (November 9, 1905), 1087.

11 Wister, *Roosevelt*, pp. 254-55.

12 Quoted in James A. Tinsley, "Roosevelt, Foraker, and the Brownsville Affray," *Journal of Negro History*, XLI (January 1956), 47, 49.

13 Quoted in Pringle, *Theodore Roosevelt*, pp. 460-61.

14 Tinsley, "Roosevelt, Foraker," 51-53. Pringle and Tinsley both contend that Foraker sought to embarrass Roosevelt and dislodge him from a position where he could choose Taft as his successor to the presidency.

15 Pringle, *Theodore Roosevelt*, pp. 462-63; Tinsley, "Roosevelt, Foraker," 61-63.

16 Monroe Nathan Work, editor, *Negro Year Book, 1912* (Tuskeegee: Negro Year Book Publishing Co., 1912), p. 30.

17 Quoted in Woodward, *Origins of the New South*, p. 468.

18 Quoted in Weyl, *Negro in American Civilization*, p. 120.

19 Woodward, *Origins of the New South*, p. 468.

20 Ira Kipnis, *The American Socialist Movement, 1897-1912* (New York: Columbia University Press, 1952), pp. 131, 134; David A. Shannon, *The Socialist Party of America* (New York: Macmillan Co., 1955), p. 52.

21 Kipnis, *American Socialist Movement*, p. 133; Debs quoted in Ray Ginger, *The Bending Cross: A Biography of Eugene V. Debs* (New Brunswick: Rutgers University Press, 1949), p. 260.

22 Quoted in Shannon, *Socialist Party*, p. 50.

23 Kipnis, *American Socialist Movement*, p. 131.

24 *Ibid.*, pp. 131-32.

25 *Ibid.*, p. 133.

26 Quoted in William E. Walling, *Progressivism—And After* (New York: Macmillan Co., 1914), pp. 377-81.

27 Walling, "Science and Human Brotherhood," 1318.

28 Kirk H. Porter and Donald Bruce Johnson, editors, *National Party Plat-forms, 1840-1956* (Urbana: The University of Illinois Press, 1956), pp. 160, 183-88.

29 Quoted in Arthur S. Link, "Theodore Roosevelt and the South," *North Carolina Historical Review*, XXIII (July 1946), 314.

30 Theodore Roosevelt, "The Progressives and the Colored Man," *Outlook*, CI (August 24, 1912), 909-12. Roosevelt was no doubt disconcerted by the fact that sixty-two black delegates from the South had voted for Taft at the Republican convention. See William F. Nowlin, *The Negro in American National Politics* (Boston: The Stratford Co., 1931), p. 56. Roosevelt's letter was widely circulated, being printed in many southern newspapers and also being used as a campaign pamphlet. The reply by Julian Harris of Atlanta, the son of Joel Chandler Harris of "Uncle Remus" fame, was not circulated, although it is most interesting. It has been reprinted by Arthur Link in the *Journal of Southern History*, X (November 1944), 488-90.

31 "Official Minutes of the (Provisional) Progressive National Committee," p. 51, Theodore Roosevelt MSS.

32 *Ibid.*, pp. 101-3, 234.

33 *Ibid.*, p. 231; "Official Minutes of the First National Convention of the Progressive Party," p. 140, Theodore Roosevelt MSS.

34 "Official Minutes of the (Provisional) Progressive National Committee," pp. 47, 238-39, 246, 250, 261, Theodore Roosevelt MSS.

35 *Ibid.*, p. 217.

36 *Ibid.*, pp. 215-16, 244, 247.

37 Franklin, *Slavery to Freedom*, p. 445.

38 "Official Minutes of the First National Convention of the Progressive Party," p. 194, Theodore Roosevelt MSS; Pinchot, *Progressive Party*, p. 195. Mowry, *Theodore Roosevelt*, p. 267, states that there was rather widespread opposition to Roosevelt's plan of a "lily-white" party from the "Garrisonian" faction. However, the minutes of the convention and Pinchot's *History of the Progressive Party* cite only Jane Addams as being in opposition.

39 George Mowry, "The South and the Progressive Lily White Party of 1912," *Journal of Southern History*, VI (May 1940), 244-45.

40 Unsigned review, "No Square Deal," *Independent*, LXXIII (August 15, 1912), 391.

41 "Progressive National Platform, 1916," Theodore Roosevelt MSS.

42 Quoted in Ray Stannard Baker, *Woodrow Wilson, Life and Letters* (Garden City: Doubleday, Doran and Co., 1931), III, 387.

43 Arthur S. Link, "The Negro as a Factor in the Campaign of 1912," *Journal of Negro History*, XXXII (January 1947), 85, 93, 98.

44 Villard, *Fighting Years*, p. 238.

45 *Ibid.*, p. 240.

46 John Morton Blum, *Woodrow Wilson and the Politics of Morality*, edited by Oscar Handlin (Boston: Little, Brown and Co., 1956), p. 115.

47 Unsigned review, "Race Discrimination in Washington," *Independent*, LXXVI (November 20, 1913), 330.

48 Link, "The Negro as a Factor in the Campaign of 1912," 87.

49 Baker, *Woodrow Wilson, Life and Letters*, IV, 222.
50 Blum, *Woodrow Wilson*, p. 116. Wilson had a lot of progressive company in opposing women's rights and suffrage. See Arthur Mann, *Yankee Reformers in the Urban League* (Cambridge: Harvard University Press, 1954), p. 211.
51 Editorial, *New Republic*, I (November 21, 1914), 5.
52 Franklin, *Slavery to Freedom*, p. 446.

CHAPTER VI

1 Archibald Grimke, "Why Disfranchisement Is Bad," *Atlantic Monthly*, XCIV (July 1904), 80-81.
2 Quoted in unsigned review, "Race Problems Knocking at the Doors of Congress," 96.
3 Claude G. Bowers, *Beveridge and the Progressive Era* (Cambridge: Houghton Mifflin Co., 1932), p. 121.
4 Quoted in Lothrop Stoddard, *The Rising Tide of Color against White World-Supremacy* (New York: Charles Scribner's Sons, 1923), p. xxx.

BIBLIOGRAPHY

1 PRIMARY SOURCES

A *Books and Manuscripts*

Abbott, Lyman. *America in the Making.* New Haven: Yale University Press, 1911.
——— *Reminiscences.* Boston: Houghton Mifflin Co., 1915.
Adams, Charles Francis, Jr. *An Autobiography.* Boston: Houghton Mifflin Co., 1916.
——— *Lee at Appomattox and Other Papers.* Second edition enlarged. Boston: Houghton Mifflin Co., 1902.
Bailey, Thomas Pearce. *Race Orthodoxy in the South.* New York: The Neale Publishing Co., 1914.

Baker, Ray Stannard. *Following the Color Line*. New York: Doubleday, Page and Co., 1908.

———— *Woodrow Wilson, Life and Letters* (Volumes III-IV). Garden City: Doubleday, Doran and Co., 1931.

Boas, Franz. *The Mind of Primitive Man*. New York: Macmillan Co., 1911.

Commons, John R. *Races and Immigrants*. New York: Macmillan Co., 1907.

Croly, Herbert. *Progressive Democracy*. New York: Macmillan Co., 1914.

———— *The Promise of American Life*. New York: Macmillan Co., 1909.

DuBois, W. E. B. *The Souls of Black Folk: Essays and Sketches*. Third edition. Chicago: A. C. McClurg & Co., 1903.

Higginson, Thomas Wentworth. *Letters and Journals of Thomas Wentworth Higginson, 1846-1906*, edited by Mary Thacher Higginson. Boston: Houghton Mifflin Co., 1921.

Hoar, George F. *Autobiography of Seventy Years* (Volume II). New York: Charles Scribner's Sons, 1903.

Howe, Frederic C. *The Confessions of a Reformer*. New York: Charles Scribner's Sons, 1925.

La Follette, Robert M. *Autobiography*. Madison: Robert M. La Follette Co., 1913.

Lippmann, Walter. *A Preface to Politics*. New York: Mitchell Kennerley, 1914.

Miller, Kelly. *Race Adjustment: Essays on the Negro in America*. New York: The Neale Publishing Co., 1908.

Ovington, Mary White. *The Walls Came Tumbling Down*. New York: Harcourt, Brace and Co., 1947.

Pinchot, Amos. *The History of the Progressive Party, 1912-1916*, edited by H. M. Hooker. New York: New York University Press, 1958.

Quillan, Frank W. *The Color Line in Ohio*. Ann Arbor: George Wahr, 1913.

102

Rauschenbusch, Walter. *Christianizing the Social Order.* New York: Macmillan Co., 1912.

Roosevelt, Theodore. *The Letters of Theodore Roosevelt* (Volumes II, VII), edited by Elting E. Morison. Cambridge: Harvard University Press, 1951.

————— Manuscript Collection in Library of Congress.

Ross, Edward A. *The Old World in the New.* New York: The Century Co., 1914.

Royce, Josiah. *Race Questions, Provincialism, and Other American Problems.* New York: Macmillan Co., 1908.

Schurz, Carl. *The Autobiography of Carl Schurz*, abridgement by Wayne Andrews. New York: Charles Scribner's Sons, 1961.

————— *Speeches, Correspondence and Political Papers*, edited by Frederic Bancroft. 6 vols. New York: G. P. Putnam's Sons, 1913.

Sumner, William Graham. *Folkways.* Boston: Ginn & Co., 1907.

Villard, Oswald Garrison. *Fighting Years: Memoirs of a Liberal Editor.* New York: Harcourt, Brace and Co., 1939.

Walling, William English. *Progressivism—And After.* New York: Macmillan Co., 1914.

Weatherford, W. D. *Negro Life in the South.* New York: Association Press, 1918.

Weyl, Walter. *The New Democracy.* New York: Macmillan Co., 1912.

White, William Allen. *The Old Order Changeth: A View of American Democracy.* New York: Macmillan Co., 1912.

————— *Selected Letters of William Allen White, 1899-1943*, edited by Walter Johnson. New York: H. Holt & Co., 1947.

Whitlock, Brand. *Forty Years of It.* New York: D. Appleton and Co., 1914.

Wilson, Woodrow. *The New Freedom*, edited by William E. Leuchtenburg. Englewood Cliffs: Prentice-Hall, Inc., 1961.

Wister, Owen. *Roosevelt, the Story of a Friendship*. New York: Macmillan Co., 1930.

B *Articles and Newspapers*

Adams, Charles Francis, Jr. "Reflex Light from Africa." *The Century Magazine*, LXXII (1906), 101-11.

Addams, Jane. "Has the Emancipation Act Been Nullified by National Indifference?" *The Survey*, XXIX (February 1, 1913), 565-66.

Atkinson, Edward. "The Negro as a Beast." *North American Review*, CLXXXI (August 1905), 202-15.

Baker, Ray Stannard. "The Color Line in the North." *American Magazine*, LXV (1908), 345-56.

———— "Negro Suffrage in a Democracy." *Atlantic Monthly*, CVI (November 1910), 612-19.

———— "What Is Lynching?" *McClure's Magazine*, XXIV (January 1905), 299-314.

Bean, Robert Bennett, M.D. "The Negro Brain." *The Century Magazine*, LXXII (1906), 778-84.

Boyle, James. "Has the Fifteenth Amendment Been Justified?" *The Arena*, XXXI (May 1904), 481-88.

Brown, William Garrott. "President Roosevelt and the South." *Independent*, LIX (November 9, 1905), 1086-89.

———— "The White Peril: The Immediate Danger of the Negro." *North American Review*, CLXXIX (1904), 824-41.

"Changed Opinions on the Race Question." *The World's Work*, V (1903), 3156-57.

Conant, William B. "The Future of the Negro." *The Arena*, XL (July 1908), 62-65.

Cutler, James Elbert. "The Practice of Lynching in the United States." *South Atlantic Quarterly*, VI (April 1907), 125-34.

(Editorial). *The American Review of Reviews*, XXVIII (August 1903), 138-39.

(Editorial). *New Republic*, I (November 21, 1914), 5.

(Editorial). *Outlook*, LXXIII (April 25, 1903), 950-52.

"Fifty Years of Freedom." *The World's Work*, XXVI (June 1913), 148-49.

Grimke, Archibald H. "Why Disfranchisement Is Bad." *Atlantic Monthly*, XCIV (July 1904), 72-81.

Hart, Albert B. "The Outcome of the Southern Race Question." *North American Review*, CLXXXVIII (July 1908), 50-61.

Hawley, Walter L. "Passing of the Race Problem." *The Arena*, XXIV (November 1900), 467-78.

Hemstreet, William. "The Problem of the Blacks." *The Arena*, XXIX (May 1903), 495-99.

"Is the Race Problem Insoluble?" *Independent*, LX (June 21, 1906), 1495-97.

Kenilworth, Walter Winston. "Negro Influence in American Life." *Forum*, XLVI (1911), 169-78.

"Lynching and Public Sentiment." *Outlook*, XCVIII (June 10, 1911), 289-90.

Mecklin, John M. "The Philosophy of the Color Line." *American Journal of Sociology*, XIX (November 1913), 343-57.

New York *Times*. 1901, 1909-1912.

New York *Tribune*. 1877.

"No Square Deal." *Independent*, LXXIII (August 15, 1912), 391-93.

Page, Thomas Nelson. "The Negro: The Southerners' Problem." *McClure's Magazine*, XXII (April 1904), 619-26.

———— "President Roosevelt from the Standpoint of a Southern Democrat." *Metropolitan Magazine*, XXI (1905), 680-81.

"The Platform of the Outlook." *Outlook*, LXXXIV (September 1, 1906), 4.

Poe, Clarence. "What Is Justice between White Man and Black Man in the Rural South?" in *Lectures and Addresses on the Negro in the South*. Charlottesville: The Michie Co., n.d., pp. 37-55.

"Race Discrimination in Washington." *Independent,* LXXVI (November 20, 1913), 330.

"Race Problems Knocking at the Doors of Congress." *Current Opinion,* LIV (February 1913), 95-97.

"The Real Interest of the Negro." *The American Review of Reviews,* XXVII (February 1903), 149.

Roosevelt, Theodore. "The Progressives and the Colored Man." *Outlook,* CI (August 24, 1912), 909-12.

Ross, Edward A. "The Causes of Race Superiority." *Annals of the American Academy of Political and Social Science,* XVIII (July 1901), 67-89.

Schurz, Carl. "Can the South Solve the Negro Problem?" *McClure's Magazine,* XXII (January 1904), 259-75.

"Secretary Taft as Conciliator." *Independent,* LXIV (March 19, 1908), 696-97.

Sledd, Andrew. "The Negro: Another View." *Atlantic Monthly,* XC (July 1902), 67-73.

Villard, Oswald Garrison. "The President and the Segregation at Washington." *North American Review,* CXCVIII (December 1913), 800-807.

Walling, William English. "The Race War in the North." *Independent,* LXV (September 3, 1908), 529-34.

———— "Science and Human Brotherhood." *Independent,* LXVI (1909), 1318-27.

"The Worst Opprest." *Independent,* LXXIII (August 22, 1912), 448.

2 SECONDARY SOURCES

A *Books and Manuscripts*

Allen, Frederick Lewis. *Only Yesterday.* New York: Harper and Row, 1931.

Blum, John Morton. *Woodrow Wilson and the Politics of Morality*, edited by Oscar Handlin. Boston: Little, Brown and Co., 1956.

Bowers, Claude G. *Beveridge and the Progressive Era.* Cambridge: Houghton Mifflin Co., 1932.

Commager, Henry Steele. *The American Mind: An Interpretation of American Thought and Character since 1880.* New Haven: Yale University Press, 1950.

Curti, Merle. *The Growth of American Thought.* Second edition. New York: Harper and Brothers, 1943.

De Santis, Vincent P. *Republicans Face the Southern Question, 1877-1897.* Baltimore: The Johns Hopkins Press, 1959.

Dictionary of American Biography. 20 vols. and XXII, Supplement Two. Edited by Dumas Malone, Allen Johnson, and Robert Livingston Schuyler. New York: Charles Scribner's Sons, 1929-1936, 1958.

Durden, Robert Franklin. *James Shepherd Pike: Republicanism and the American Negro, 1850-1882.* Durham: Duke University Press, 1957.

Faulkner, Harold Underwood. *The Quest for Social Justice, 1898-1914.* New York: Macmillan Co., 1937.

Forcey, Charles. *The Crossroads of Liberalism.* New York: Oxford University Press, 1961.

Franklin, John Hope. *From Slavery to Freedom: A History of American Negroes.* New York: Alfred A. Knopf, 1948.

Fuess, Claude Moore. *Carl Schurz, Reformer.* Port Washington: Kennikat Press, Inc., 1963.

Gabriel, Ralph Henry. *The Course of American Democratic Thought.* New York: The Ronald Press Co., 1940.

Garraty, John A. *Henry Cabot Lodge.* New York: Alfred A. Knopf, 1953.

Ginger, Ray. *The Bending Cross: A Biography of Eugene V. Debs.* New Brunswick: Rutgers University Press, 1949.

Goldman, Eric. *Rendezvous with Destiny: A History of Modern American Reform.* First edition. New York: Alfred A. Knopf, 1952.

Gossett, Thomas F. *Race: The History of an Idea in America.* Dallas: Southern Methodist University Press, 1963.

Hofstadter, Richard. *The Age of Reform: From Bryan to F. D. R.* First edition. New York: Alfred A. Knopf, 1955.

———— *Social Darwinism in American Thought, 1860-1915.* Philadelphia: University of Pennsylvania Press, 1944.

Howe, M. A. DeWolfe. *Portrait of an Independent: Moorfield Storey, 1845-1929.* Boston: Houghton Mifflin Co., 1932.

Jarrell, Hampton M. *Wade Hampton and the Negro.* Columbia: University of South Carolina Press, 1950.

Kipnis, Ira. *The American Socialist Movement, 1897-1912.* New York: Columbia University Press, 1952.

Kolko, Gabriel. *The Triumph of Conservatism: A Reinterpretation of American History, 1900-1916.* London: The Free Press of Glencoe, 1963.

Lewinson, Paul. *Race, Class, and Party.* New York: Oxford University Press, 1932.

Link, Arthur S. *Woodrow Wilson and the Progressive Era.* New York: Harper and Brothers, 1954.

Logan, Rayford W. *The Negro in American Life and Thought: The Nadir, 1877-1901.* New York: The Dial Press, 1954.

McDuffie, Jerome A. "The Wilmington Riots of November 10, 1898." Unpublished master's thesis, Wake Forest College, 1963.

Mann, Arthur. *Yankee Reformers in the Urban League.* Cambridge: Harvard University Press, 1954.

Maxwell, Robert S. *La Follette and the Rise of the Progressives in Wisconsin.* Madison: State Historical Society of Wisconsin, 1956.

Mowry, George E. *The Era of Theodore Roosevelt, 1900-1912.* New York: Harper and Brothers, 1958.

———— *Theodore Roosevelt and the Progressive Movement.* Madison: The University of Wisconsin Press, 1947.

Nowlin, William F. *The Negro in American National Politics.* Boston: The Stratford Co., 1931.

Nye, Russel B. *Midwestern Progressive Politics.* Lansing: Michigan State University Press, 1959.

Porter, Kirk H., and Donald Bruce Johnson, editors. *National Party Platforms, 1840-1956.* Urbana: The University of Illinois Press, 1956.

Pringle, Henry F. *The Life and Times of William Howard Taft* (Volume II). New York: Farrar & Rinehart, Inc., 1939.

———— *Theodore Roosevelt: A Biography.* New York: Harcourt, Brace and Co., 1931.

Regier, C. C. *The Era of the Muckrakers.* Chapel Hill: The University of North Carolina Press, 1932.

Shannon, David A. *The Socialist Party of America.* New York: Macmillan Co., 1955.

Smith, Samuel Denny. *The Negro in Congress, 1870-1901.* Chapel Hill: The University of North Carolina Press, 1940.

Southern Race Commission on the Study of Lynching. *Lynchings and What They Mean.* Atlanta: The Commission, 1931.

Spencer, Samuel R., Jr. *Booker T. Washington and the Negro's Place in American Life.* Boston: Little, Brown and Co., 1955.

Stampp, Kenneth M. *The Era of Reconstruction, 1865-1877.* New York: Alfred A. Knopf, 1965.

Stoddard, Lothrop. *The Rising Tide of Color against White World-Supremacy.* New York: Charles Scribner's Sons, 1923.

Stone, Irving. *Clarence Darrow for the Defense.* New York: Doubleday Co., 1941.

Sweet, William Warren. *Makers of Christianity* (Volume III). New York: H. Holt & Co., 1937.

Tindall, George Brown. *South Carolina Negroes, 1877-1900*. Columbia: University of South Carolina Press, 1952.

Wesley, Charles H. *Negro Labor in the United States, 1850-1925*. New York: Vanguard Press, 1927.

Weyl, Nathaniel. *The Negro in American Civilization*. Washington: Public Affairs Press, 1960.

Wiebe, Robert H. *Businessmen and Reform: A Study of the Progressive Movement*. Cambridge: Harvard University Press, 1962.

Woodward, C. Vann. *Origins of the New South, 1877-1913*. Volume IX of *A History of the South*, edited by Wendell Holmes Stephenson and E. Merton Coulter. Baton Rouge: Louisiana State University Press, 1951.

———— *Reunion and Reaction*. First edition. Boston: Little, Brown and Co., 1951.

———— *The Strange Career of Jim Crow*. New York: Oxford University Press, 1957.

Work, Monroe Nathan, editor. *Negro Year Book, 1912*. Tuskeegee: Negro Year Book Publishing Co., 1912.

B *Articles*

Brown, Ira V. "Lyman Abbott and Freedmen's Aid." *Journal of Southern History*, XV (February 1949), 22-38.

Cook, Raymond A. "The Man Behind 'The Birth of a Nation.' " *North Carolina Historical Review*, XXXIX (Autumn 1962), 519-40.

Davis, Allen F. "The Social Workers and the Progressive Party, 1912-1916." *American Historical Review*, LXIX (April 1964), 671-88.

Dexter, Byron. "Herbert Croly and the Promise of American Life." *Political Science Quarterly*, LXX (June 1955), 197-218.

Grantham, Dewey W., Jr. "Hoke Smith, Progressive Governor of Georgia, 1907-1909." *Journal of Southern History*, XV (November 1949), 423-40.

Leuchtenburg, William E. "Progressivism and Imperialism: The Progressive Movement and Foreign Policy, 1898-1916." *Mississippi Valley Historical Review*, XXXIX (December 1952), 483-504.

Link, Arthur S. "Correspondence Relating to the Progressive Party's 'Lily-White' Policy in 1912." *Journal of Southern History*, X (November 1944), 488-90.

———— "The Negro as a Factor in the Campaign of 1912." *Journal of Negro History*, XXXII (January 1947), 81-99.

———— "Theodore Roosevelt and the South." *North Carolina Historical Review*, XXIII (July 1946), 313-24.

Mabry, W. A. "Disfranchisement of the Negro in Mississippi." *Journal of Southern History*, IV (August 1938), 322.

Matthews, Fred H. "White Community and 'Yellow Peril.'" *Mississippi Valley Historical Review*, L (March 1964), 612-33.

Mowry, George E. "The South and the Progressive Lily White Party of 1912." *Journal of Southern History*, VI (May 1940), 237-47.

Scheiner, Seth M. "Theodore Roosevelt and the Negro, 1901-1908." *Journal of Negro History*, XLVII (July 1962), 176.

Tinsley, James A. "Roosevelt, Foraker, and the Brownsville Affray." *Journal of Negro History*, XLI (January 1956), 43-65.

Welch, Richard E., Jr. "The Federal Election Bill of 1890: Postscripts and Prelude." *The Journal of American History*, LII (December 1965), 511.

Woodward, C. Vann. "Tom Watson and the Negro in Agrarian Politics." *Journal of Southern History*, IV (February 1938), 14-33.

INDEX

116